THE BIG SCALE BACK

Success and balance by your own design

Edited by Kelly Lamb and Christine Stock
Interior design and typesetting by Doris Chung
Cover design by Michelle Fairbanks

Author Photo by Dom Productions

TORONTO

THE BIG SCALE BACK

Success and balance by your own design

STEPHANIE WOODWARD

To Terry—here's to our scaled back life.

TABLE OF CONTENTS

MOVING FROM UNCONSCIOUS PRODUCTIVITY TO CONSCIOUS PRODUCTIVITY

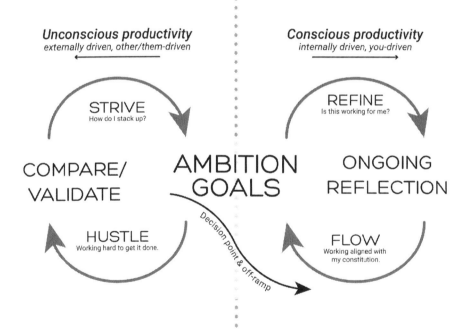

Unconscious productivity
externally driven, other/them-driven

Conscious productivity
internally driven, you-driven

STRIVE
How do I stack up?

REFINE
Is this working for me?

COMPARE/
VALIDATE

AMBITION
GOALS

ONGOING
REFLECTION

HUSTLE
Working hard to get it done.

FLOW
Working aligned with
my constitution.

Decision point & off-ramp

UNCONSCIOUS PRODUCTIVITY

Work is all-encompassing for so many of us. **Not only does it take up space and time in our lives, it shapes and influences how we go about *living* our lives.** Work impacts:

- When we sleep and when we're awake
- How, when, and what we eat
- How and when we parent our children
- Where we choose to live
- Our finances
- Our identities
- Our energy levels
- Our moods
- Our workout times
- When we socialize
- When we relax

It's not just the time we're "on the clock" that can take over our lives—work weaves its way in to so many aspects and layers of our lives, whether we're aware of its impact or not.

How you earn money and how you approach your work dictates how you live your life. So, we all need to be thinking very consciously about our relationship with work. I've been a leadership and life coach for almost a decade, and my work with clients is anchored in how they approach their work. They come into coaching with a work-related objective: craving a career change, searching for a feeling of fulfillment with how they're earning money or where they work, wanting to manage interpersonal dynamics at work or their feelings of disillusionment or exhaustion.

While the subject that draws them to coaching is a specific career-related objective, inevitably the coaching goes much deeper than that. What I've learned from my own journey and working with my clients is that **it's our *relationship* with work that needs attention, rather than any specific issue.**

This book outlines both a framework that you can work your way through *and* my own personal journey as a lived example of the framework. While it shares my specific path, I suspect that the themes and issues I faced will resonate with many of you. I had to confront beliefs I simply absorbed—from family, teachers, friends, colleagues, and society—that I had allowed to drive my decisions about my path in life and how I earned money. I then made the conscious decision to change *how* I earned money—choosing to abandon the 24/7, frenzied, smartphone-addicted way of working that just didn't serve me.

We're often conditioned to believe that we need to sacrifice so many elements of our personal lives to climb the corporate ladder. I'll share why I am done with living that way—*and yet I'm just as committed to successful outcomes and results.* We don't need to over-identify with work and hyper-productivity to be successful. We don't need to wear over-productivity as a badge of honor.

My ambition, work ethic, and true love of work had me showing up in the workplace eager, dedicated, and engaged. But over time, I felt my personal fulfillment and satisfaction waning, despite achieving success by all external measures. A blend of people pleasing, a need for external validation, conditioning, and fear had me dressing up in what felt like a costume, participating in meetings that felt cold and formal, and whizzing through my days as if powered by adrenaline. I was rewarded, promoted, and beloved by my bosses and organizations. I was always available, always on alert, always wearing my hyper-vigilance and responsibility like a cape that would protect me from the deep feelings of dissatisfaction that I pushed down daily, along with my desire for joy and a well-rounded, fulfilling life.

Like so many, work also formed a big part of my identity. It felt like the only part of my life I could control. And after having spent years studying and striving and reaching for the top of the class, then climbing corporate ladders, what would it say about me to question the traditional definitions of success and ambition? There was an undercurrent of that operating within me for a long time. I had been taught that to care about work and to be ambitious meant placing work above all else. I never wanted to be perceived as ungrateful. And

I certainly didn't want to be perceived as lazy. It took me years—many, many years!—to finally learn about balance and rethink how I was approaching my life, both professionally and personally. It's what led me to my own experiment in creating work–life fulfillment: the big scale back.

We bring a lot into our workplaces: beliefs about ourselves, about what "success" means and looks like, as well as our work ethic. I wrote this book to help others recognize that finding work–life fulfillment doesn't mean quitting, becoming lazy, or abandoning your dreams and ambition. Quite the opposite. Since "scaling back," I've built a thriving business and written a book, all while taking the time to savor and enjoy the rest of my life. **There is a way to be both successful and happy, to have balance and joy—at work and in every other aspect of your life.**

UNCONSCIOUS PRODUCTIVITY

If *productivity* is the state of producing something and *unconscious* is that part of our mind that is inaccessible to the conscious mind (but that affects our behavior and emotions), what do you get when you put them together? **You get us humans rushing about like worker bees, producing, and getting things done without thinking about the emotions and behaviors that underpin that busyness.**

Have a look at the left-hand side of the graphic on page 1, *Unconscious Productivity*. Most of us will spend our entire lives on this left-hand side: setting goals that are shaped by external factors (society, parents, friends, siblings, spouses, partners, or any influential "others" in our lives), and then hustling and striving in service of those externally driven goals. It can lead to a continuous loop of comparison, hustle, and an ongoing feeling of unfulfillment and not enough-ness.

Unconscious productivity can sound like this:

My parents always wanted me to be a . . .
I want to be able to afford nice things and provide my kids with more than I had, so I need to . . .
I need to show that I'm as talented as my brother/sister . . .
So-and-so is already running a company; I should be too . . .

When we peel back the layers, all kinds of factors *external to ourselves* are running the show. **This is *unconscious productivity*, and in my experience, it's the cause of disillusionment, dissatisfaction, and unfulfillment because we're living our professional lives guided by the values and expectations of *others* rather than according to our own inner compass.**

CONSCIOUS PRODUCTIVITY

Now take a look at the right-hand side of the graphic on page 1. *Conscious productivity* is about success, ambition, and productivity rooted in an understanding of *yourself*. Remove external expectation, external conditioning, and the opinions of *others*, and uncover what it is that you want to be doing and the environment in which *you* want to be doing it. When you are able to honor your own values and your own ideal conditions—your own *truth*—you'll show up in the professional world authentically, which is when and how you can do your best work.

Once you understand what it is you truly want and need, you can go about setting clear boundaries, defining your values, and honoring your true nature, just as I now honor my need to live in line with my values, my true nature, and the work I feel called to do in this world. I'll be sharing both a framework and my personal stories to bring the concepts to life. These stories are obviously my stories, so the goals, beliefs, and learnings that I share are unique to me. Your experience and story will, of course, be unique to you. But the framework and the principles I will share can be applied to anyone and can help you build a life by your own design.

UNRAVELING BELIEFS

Throughout this book, I'm going to share the obstacles we all encounter when we embark on personal change (spoiler: it's not always easy, and it almost always feels uncomfortable, especially when that change is related to work). You'll learn how to move from battling, resisting, and pushing against these obstacles to understanding, accepting, and moving past them by deepening your conscious awareness, shifting your mindset, and owning what is true for *you*.

This framework, this process, is about deepening your self-awareness and learning to tune in to your own inner compass, and giving yourself permission to evolve and grow. To change your mind—and your path—when you uncover something new about yourself.

This journey of mine was centered around work, ambition, and productivity. As I started to unravel my beliefs about myself, about ambition, about productivity, and about hustle, I learned that most of these beliefs had been conditioned into me—as many of our beliefs are—by all those influential people around me: parents, teachers, bosses, friends, and broader family members. That conditioning and those beliefs turned into patterns of behavior and influenced the choices I made about my career—and how I approached my work. Those patterns of behavior became "just the way I do things." In other words, I was approaching it all *unconsciously*.

In my family, we rarely rested—there was always a go-go mentality. Sleeping in or just lounging about was most definitely considered *lazy*. From an early age, I internalized getting things done as appropriate, desired behavior, regardless of whether I felt tired or in need of rest. On the positive side, this upbringing gifted me with a good level of resilience and "stick-with-it-ness." I think I have yet to miss a deadline in life! However, this came with a cost. It also led me to lose touch with my own internal warning signs and guideposts. I would override and power through exhaustion from working eighty-plus hours per week with caffeine, rather than rest. My adrenals paid the price.

At different work places, hours in front of the computer or early mornings and late nights were equated with a good work ethic and dedication to the organization. Those who were at their computers longer were deemed more desirable employees. I internalized this, and—despite being the type of person who works best in intense bursts and sprints—I adopted the practice of logging hours in front of the computer and being endlessly available. The upside? I rose up the ranks quickly. The downside? I still worked intensely as though I was in a sprint even though I was actually in a marathon. Again, my adrenals paid the price.

I *unconsciously* adopted beliefs and allowed those beliefs to shape my thoughts and my actions. Those beliefs, which were shaped by others around me, determined my path. It was only as I started to unravel the conditioning that I discovered that my constitution, my gifts, my talents, and ultimately my ambition and life dreams were unique to me (and different to what my conditioning had led me to believe). And that what I *really* needed was to understand and learn from my own experience with myself. I needed to decide what really worked for *me* and to do the work to put that into practice by making decisions about my career, my relationships, and my life that aligned with that knowing.

This is the path of *conscious productivity*. That word "conscious" can sound mystical and a little woo-woo, can't it? I hummed and hawed over language for this work, and time and time again, I came back to "conscious." The definition of this word is simple: *having knowledge of something; aware of.* And that really gets at the purpose of this book: I want you to become more self-aware and to deepen your knowledge and awareness of your relationship with productivity.

This is the conscious productivity framework and philosophy that

I use in my coaching practice, and with my clients. It draws on everything I've learned, but perhaps most importantly, it's what my clients have put into practice to design their own lives. To understand what it is they *truly* want from their work lives and how their work lives connect to all other areas of life.

LIMITING BELIEFS—YOUR EARLIEST PROGRAMMING

How often do you feel really certain about something? Like, what's right or wrong; what's good or bad; what's appropriate or inappropriate?

There are certain things that may fall into objective categories. For example, many of us would agree that stealing is wrong, damaging someone's property is bad, and that wearing a warm jacket in sub-zero temperatures is appropriate.

But then there are all those other times, when something that we feel really certain about is, in fact, simply a subjective belief we hold. For example, wearing a suit to work is appropriate; working long hours is noble; and business meetings are good.

These are all examples of core beliefs. ***Core beliefs* are foundational thoughts and assumptions that you have about yourself and the world around you.** And they impact every aspect of your life, from your self-image to your relationships, to how you approach your work.

Some of these beliefs are universal and can serve us well. And the fact that these beliefs operate on autopilot can save us a lot of mental energy. Imagine if you had to go through your day contemplating every single action and behavior as though you were doing it for the first time. It would be draining and exhausting. So there is a place for these beliefs to minimize mental drain, conserve energy, and to help us make effective, quick decisions.

However, it can also contribute to significant bias in our own lives and create mental ruts and habits of thought at times when it may serve us best to think differently or challenge our preconceived notions. There are many dangerous consequences of these core beliefs. For example, racism stems from core beliefs that lead to outwardly directed bias. For the purposes of this book, though, we'll be focused on *inwardly directed* core beliefs. That is, how your core beliefs have shaped how you feel about yourself, and how they influence your actions and decisions. Specifically, how they may be limiting you in your own life when it comes to your beliefs around work, ambition, and productivity.

Limiting beliefs are a type of _core belief_. They are core beliefs that you have about yourself that limit or restrict you in some way. They are tricky because *you believe them to be objective truth* when, in fact, they are subjective, unconscious beliefs that you have formed over your lifetime. Once these beliefs are formed, they create the parameters for your life. The word "limiting" is there for a reason. They place limits on what you think is possible for you and how you can live your life. They fence you in and trick you into believing that the territory you can "play" in is much smaller than it actually is.

These beliefs are formed in different ways: from your childhood and how you were parented, to your specific experiences (including everything from your exposure to the media, to cultural experiences), through to your natural disposition. Over time, they become firmly held ideas that you have about yourself, other people, the world, and your future. Remember the left-hand side of the graphic on page 1? Your core limiting beliefs keep you in the goal-hustle-strive-compare loop of *unconscious productivity*.

Here are some examples from my clients over the years:

I'm not good enough for that job.
If I'm not producing, I'm not valuable.
I can make good money if I just work really hard.
Too much money corrupts.
Money will bring me happiness.
It's not possible to be a great parent and a great employee.
I'm too old to make a career change now.

These are all limiting beliefs, and they served to hold my clients back in different ways and influenced their outcomes, and what they believed was possible for them. For example, the client who believed having too much money could have negative outcomes ended up struggling with money blocks, which resulted in keeping them stuck at a very specific salary level. The client who believed money would bring them happiness could never earn enough to find that happiness, which drove them to earn more and more and miss out on the other experiences in their life.

Some of your limiting beliefs about work may have been formed in childhood, well before you entered the workforce. You may have observed your parents or guardians behaving a certain way, and you began modeling their behaviors in your own life. Or perhaps your parents were explicit about what they believed was right for you or what they expected of you, and you internalized that as the true, right path for you. Then as you moved from childhood to adulthood, you took in perspectives from others who may have been influential to you, including teachers, friends, and bosses. Your unconscious registered information from all of these sources, and it contributed to the formation of your own unconscious beliefs—ones that you still hold today—both those that serve you and those that limit you. Over time, those beliefs became truth in your mind and drove—and continue to drive—your thoughts, actions, and decisions.

And here's the damaging part: because we hold these limiting beliefs as truth, they often go unnoticed and unchallenged in our own minds. After all, why would we question what we hold as true? And if you aren't questioning and challenging these beliefs, how on earth would you be aware of them, let alone change them? These then become our core beliefs.

In fact, it gets even worse: once you establish these core beliefs, you can end up falling prey to confirmation bias, meaning that you tend to pay attention to evidence and experiences that reinforce your beliefs, and pay less attention to evidence or experiences that disprove them or goes contrary to them. In this way, **your core limiting beliefs can become self-fulfilling prophecies.**

This is where the *unconscious to conscious productivity* journey begins—identifying your limiting beliefs about work, ambition, and productivity. We're going to bring them out of the shadows and shine a big bright light on them to expose them for what they are—**beliefs that get in the way of you fulfilling your potential, operating at your best, and living a life that feels fulfilling to you.**

You'll identify those beliefs, and I'll ask you to face them, challenge them, and question their validity. Imagine if those beliefs are holding you back from fulfillment across all areas of your life? Imagine what might be possible then.

Why do we start with core beliefs?

Because before you can create sustainable change in your life and create the conditions for something new, you need to understand why you're doing what you're doing that is creating your current circumstances. To understand what current beliefs are driving your current behaviors, actions, and outcomes.

Moving your core beliefs from *unconscious to conscious* changes everything. This is the foundational work for transformational change and making real, sustainable, fulfilling change in your life. **Your core beliefs form your identity, and your identity drives your behaviors, habits, and actions.** To change them takes conscious effort, patience, time, and eventually deliberate behavior change, which is where we're headed in this book. This is how you will move from *unconscious productivity* to *conscious productivity*.

* * *

My relationship with work, ambition, hustle, and productivity formed young. I think I was born with an innate love of learning. Some of my earliest memories revolve around books, stories, and seeking out new experiences. That delight and glee in learning something new, listening to and eventually reading through a new bedtime book, was something I craved and yearned for.

Then school began, and that natural delight and love of learning was soon mixed in with something else: measurement, expectation, and defined purpose.

The glee and pure delight was soon tempered by other questions: What am I reading and learning this *for*? How *well* am I learning and reading it? And what am I going to *do* with this new information?

And then, of course, report cards entered my universe. These slips of paper were some of the earliest measures and critical data that my little mind used to help me answer those questions. These slips of paper that were doled out three times per year became identity measures for me. They became the opportunity to prove that I was worthy of celebration and special treatment. Not at first, of course. I had no idea these slips of paper could hold such magic. At first they were just letters and words jotted down on a page by the teachers. But I learned quickly that those letters were worth a whole lot more.

I remember my parents, my dad specifically, poring over them, beaming. One letter, A, had especially big power. A page dotted with A's resulted in all kinds of accolades; I'd get scooped up, hugged, and told how proud he was of me.

I remember one particularly good one. As had become tradition, I waited by the kitchen island at 7:30 p.m., knowing he would walk through the door any minute. We'd grab a snack, I'd pass him my report card, and we'd head down to the bar in the basement (yes, you read that correctly: my parents had an English-style bar built in our basement).

As predicted, at 7:36 p.m., Dad pushed through the door, his briefcase hand curled around the handle while nudging the mudroom door forward with his other hand, rattling the house keys free from the lock. He dropped everything as I ran over to him and threw myself into his awaiting hug.

"I have my report card!" I exclaimed, waving it above my head.

He loosened his tie and undid the top collar button of his shirt with the same two fingers. He tousled my hair and said with a wink, "Let me get changed, and I'll meet you you-know-where with you-know-what."

I put a hand over my mouth to stifle a giggle. Grabbing the stash of chips and nut mixture, I ran to the basement.

About a year prior, my parents had transformed our cement-and-cold-storage basement into their very own private English pub with a billiards table, dart board, shuffleboard, and full-scale stocked bar. There was even a street lantern and bench as part of the decor. It was my dad's oasis, that den and bar. He'd come home and head straight for it. That night was different, though, because I had a reason to be down there with him and had something important to talk to him about. He stood behind the bar in his track pants and zippered sweatshirt shaking the silver martini shaker. It always made me giggle because he'd shake his hips and whistle whatever tune came to his mind as he did it. As he poured the contents into a martini glass, frosted perfectly, he looked up at me. "And what can I get for you, young lady?"

Rolling my eyes to the ceiling and poking my index finger into my cheek, I pretended to think about it. "Coca-Cola Classic on the rocks!" I exclaimed, and with a definitive nod, I added, "with a twist." And he would then pretend to shake my drink in the shaker and pour it over a pile of ice nestled in a lowball glass, resting a lemon wedge on the edge of the glass.

He passed it to me across the bar, then walked around to sit in the barstool next to me. I sat sipping my Coca-Cola, my 11-year-old feet dangling and swinging because they couldn't reach the foot rest on the barstool. "So, walk me through these," he said, putting on his glasses and holding the report card out in front of him.

And so I did, in painstaking detail. The extra homework I'd done in Ms. Preston's class that she referenced in her notes, which had led to the A+ rating. My perseverance in the track and field unit, despite my hatred of shot put and running long jump. My love of fractions and percentages. "That A was easy because I loved it," I remarked, pointing at the letter on the page. My heart raced a bit more as he approached the English class comments. "I wrote a full short story!" I exclaimed, not able to wait for him to digest the teacher's comments himself. She'd spoken of a natural gift I had for language and creative writing. Never had a comment thrilled me as much as that one.

"Mm-hmm," he said as he continued to skim over the comments. His finger landed back next to the math grade. "Well done." He put one arm around me and gave me a big kiss on the cheek. "A top up?" he asked, reaching for my empty glass. The half-squeezed lemon wedge sat perched on what remained of the three ice cubes. I didn't mention the short story again, just nodded my head for the refill. I reminded myself that math *was* interesting, and I did enjoy the fraction unit.

As we sat there sipping our drinks, I swung my legs back and forth and poked at the ice cubes with my straw. I stared at that piece of paper between us. Amid the confusion of Grade 5 politics, the teasing from boys (*does John like me, or does he just want to hit me in the head with that scrunched piece of paper?*), the friendship rivalries (*will Jennifer still be talking to me tomorrow, or will Katie be her new best friend?*), it felt like I had no way of knowing where I ranked with anything. I didn't know whether friend groups would be the same today as they were tomorrow, whether I was "cool," or honestly, whether anything about me was "normal."

But this report card was documented proof, an indisputable ranking. It was an identity that could be proven. I could hold myself against the standard of those letter rankings for each class. I knew what I was working toward, what I aspired to, and how I was doing against that benchmark. This mattered. My dad's face and words said so. And best of all, it was an identity that I could control. I just had to keep studying, keep working, and keep performing because if I was smart and successful, I mattered. I slurped the last of my Coke, dramatically sucking in the last bit, and placed the empty glass on the bar in front of me with a satisfying thud.

* * *

My parents moved from England to Canada a year before I was born. It was intended to be a relatively short stay. "An adventure to another country!" is how my dad apparently sold my mum on the idea. She left behind a job as a law professor at a local community college and knew that her law training wouldn't transfer to Canada. It was an opportunity for Dad to grow his career in a country that seemingly offered much more opportunity to those who were smart, but hadn't been born into well-to-do families with well-established surnames. In Canada, my dad said, you could get ahead based on merit, not your father's connections. He was a man of big ambition and a belief that—within the right environment—he could make any professional dream of his come true.

And so off they went to Canada. My dad's career took off, as he built his reputation in management consulting. Mum, on the other hand, became pregnant almost immediately after they emigrated and never returned to work. Canada became their permanent new home and they now each had their role: my dad's was to earn money; my mum's was to take care of (literally) everything else.

And so it was that Mum became the day-to-day runner of lives: my dad's, my own, and my sister's. Planner, chef, professional business wife, home renovator, launderer, financial planner, cleaner, ironer, chauffeur, office manager, and travel agent. She did it all while Dad climbed the ranks at work. With Mum handling everything else, Dad was able to focus exclusively on two things: himself and his big brainy ideas.

We didn't see much of him. He traveled a lot and logged long hours at the office. Here's what I observed as a child: My dad was a business executive first, and he was an active father when he could be. And when he *could be,* wow, was he awesome. He was all kinds of fun. But getting his attention for any length of time was completely conditional on whether work was done and if his own needs were met. Those often (dare I say, always) came first.

What made Dad's absence and conditional parenting possible was my mum. Whatever the school day brought—the test mark or the schoolyard drama—Mum would greet my sister and me with a smile and a series of questions when we got home, gently pulling from us the stories of the day. Her daughters were good, hardworking, loving little humans, and she had an unwavering faith and trust that whatever we did, we were without a doubt bringing our very best. As though it were a given. This belief was stitched into the very fabric of her being, and she pulled that thread gently and meticulously every day to stitch it into ours as well. So whether through deliberate creation or natural disposition, that is what we were: good, hardworking, loving little humans who showed up earnestly and diligently every day, pencils in hand, ready to do our very best.

While Mum tended to the day-to-day ritual of raising us diligent, focused little humans, Dad loved the big moments, especially the pomp and circumstance. Report cards, recitals, and big sporting events. Those moments that were documented proof of his daughters' over-achievement. He didn't care much for the mundane and ordinariness of daily living.

* * *

Business entertaining was a big deal in the '80s and my mum excelled at the corporate dinner party. Hosting bosses, colleagues, and clients was a regular weekend occurrence. She'd pore over her *Bon Appétit* magazines, searching for new and impressive recipes that would challenge her ever-evolving culinary talents. Rumor had it that when she had married my dad, she couldn't even boil an egg. I always had a hard time believing that as I watched her whip up crêpe Suzette and pavlova on Saturday afternoons. I'd be her helper in the kitchen, standing on the step stool next to her at the kitchen island, reading out the ingredient list from the magazine that sat propped in the plastic recipe stand: "Two ozens of . . ." I'd declare in earnest and Mum would gently interrupt with a smile. "Ounces . . ." she'd correct.

I looked back at the abbreviated "oz.," puzzled.

When the cooking preparations were done, Mum moved on to the cleaning of the house and the setting of the table. Candles and flowers as centerpieces, fancy plates, and silverware. Every detail mattered to her. Her dinner parties and hostess skills were revered and unmatched.

She'd then take a long bath, choose her outfit, and descend downstairs about thirty minutes before guests were due to arrive. This was the cue for my sister and me to make ourselves scarce, which we enjoyed. It meant we could play with our toys and watch TV, without interruption. But most importantly, it gave me the opportunity to listen in on the dinner conversation.

Adult conversation fascinated me. I was convinced big, meaningful, unknown things were discussed after 8 p.m. around those dinner tables. And I wanted to know it all. The best eavesdropping point in our home growing up was the fourth step from the top of the stairs, peeking through the banisters. I tiptoed from the upstairs landing to that fourth step, unheard and unnoticed. I'd sit for hours in this spot when my parents hosted dinner parties. Sneaking out from my room and getting into position long after my mum had dashed up in between courses to tuck me into bed. By this point, I knew where all the creaks on the first three stairs were and, avoiding them, I'd crouch down on the fourth. I'd pull my knees up to my chest and stretch my nightgown up over my knees and down to my feet.

Not that the creaks on the stairs really mattered. The sounds of Billy Joel's "Uptown Girl," Lionel Richie's "Ballerina Girl," or Rod Stewart's "Maggie May" would have drowned out the sound of any staircase creak anyway. The music also made it much tougher for me to hear the conversations from my room. It had required stealth. Hence the fourth step bannister stakeout point.

This particular spot on the stairs was in the curve in the staircase, where the stairs swooped around to the right before connecting to the second floor landing. Positioned carefully, I could lean forward, peek out, and was not visible from the dining room or living room. The curve was also in the shadows—the middle space between the darkness of the upstairs and the fully lit main floor foyer. So as long as I stayed silent, no one would realize I was there. I was convinced it was only a matter of time before I heard something earth-shattering. Or learned the secrets of adult life. That nugget of information that would help me move into their adult world and leave the stressful world of childhood behind.

Adults had it made, after all. They didn't have tests; they didn't have bedtimes. They didn't have to go to school at a specific time; they didn't have to learn things they weren't interested in. No one seemed to fight—people would come to our house, laugh, drink, and chat. They could eat whatever they wanted, whenever they wanted. They could put a card into a machine and money would come out. And they could buy whatever they wanted.

I wanted in on that world. And any day now, from this hideaway on the stairs, I was going to learn the secret. As much as I tried to focus on their words, though, I'd get distracted just watching them. They'd reach for wine glasses as they giggled. The women all looked so glamorous, their shoulders all puffed out, their eyes framed in blue eyeshadow, and best of all, they all wore long and dangly or big and hooped earrings.

My mum was always the most glamorous. This particular night she was wearing a white suede jumpsuit. Oh, how I coveted that jumpsuit. I wanted to be tall enough and old enough to step into that jumpsuit.

The pant portion was pleated, and then cinched in at the waist. The top was long sleeved with a deep V-neck, the white suede speckled with patches of cerulean blue suede, as well as gold and silver brushed leather. Small metal circles studded the patches. Her collarbone-length black-brown hair was curled and teased up and around her head, brushed back around the ears to highlight the clip-on oversized tri-angular earrings.

This was my parents' Friday and Saturday night. Either at home or away. Dinner parties, drinks, laughter. They looked happy, glamorous, relaxed. Dad had usually worked an eighty-hour week, and his job for those parties was simply to show up, pour the drinks, and choose the music. Mum took care of the rest: bringing out course after course, happily refusing help from the guests. She'd sip her drink and take it all in, delighting in having delighted the crowd.

And I'd stay perched on the fourth step, watching it all—this group of management consultants and their spouses living their best lives, just having a great time. Seemingly without a care in the world. And I remember consciously documenting as I sat on those stairs: *If this is management consulting, sign me up.*

* * *

In high school, my closet overflowed with past journals. Journals I'd kept since the fifth grade, documenting my daily outpourings of emotional outrage, uncertainties, and desires. Some days, it was a few sentences; other days, it felt like the entire journal itself wasn't enough to capture the never-ending whirl of the roller coaster that was my inner world.

Our home was one of three emotions: happy, mad, and sad. And for the most part, we preferred it if no tears were shed, and anger was usually reserved for the men. So the expectation was to find and live in the happy. And to be happy. And so it was my journal that held the rageful words and the teardrops—with stains on the pages to prove it—captured behind the closed door of my bedroom, further buried behind the clothes in my closet. That was where my emotions lived.

The only ones with a window into this world were my English teachers, who were the readers and evaluators of my short stories, poetry, and essay assignments. Inspiration for all of these came from the words in my journal, and so I would pull a journal from the closet, source my feelings, and let the words pour out.

I remember hearing people talk about what they wanted to do when they grew up. I found it a funny and odd question given my upbringing. There was obviously only one real job: business. Clearly, no one else had been listening in on the adult dinner party conversations like I had. Deals, bonuses, clients, deadlines, contracts. That was the ticket to Saturday night dinner parties, laughter, and white suede jumpsuits. And what more was there to aspire to than that?

So when my English teachers would encourage me to enter my poems and short stories into contests—to which I always said no, I was way too embarrassed to let those emotional scribblings be on public display—I didn't think much of it. When they spoke to me about considering a university major in English, perhaps thinking of an MFA, it just didn't fit within my worldview. Writing stories was a pastime, clearly. I didn't know a single real-life writer; and I'd never heard my parents speak about writers or MFAs.

And so, final year of high school was filled with chemistry, biology, calculus, algebra, and geometry. My writing was pushed to the side, the journals wedged further into the closet, and poems scribbled haphazardly in the margins of notebooks on study breaks. A haiku popping up next to a parabola.

Those haikus, those poems I'd scribble, conjured up something within me—something I only felt in spurts, in between the part-time job at the pool, the algebra equations, and the periodic table of the elements—and it took me long into adulthood to recognize that the "conjured up something" was joy. That there was a heck a lot of joy stuffed and hidden in the back of that childhood closet.

And so it began—ignoring that inner desire, that inner compass of mine that *knew* and *felt* that writing and reading were areas of joy, passion, and talent for me. They fell outside of what I deemed appropriate and acceptable. I wasn't consciously pushing them aside at that point; those subjects legitimately and literally felt impossible to pursue. I wasn't aware that my inner compass was trying to speak to me, to orient me. *More of this; you love THIS!* it was trying to say. But my mental construct at the time simply shut it out.

* * *

My childhood was loving, caring, nurturing, and essentially pain- and struggle-free. Perhaps that is why my parents' perspectives and viewpoints became enmeshed with my own, without question, from a very early age.

They were the authority, of course, but it never felt like authority. It felt like loving guidance. And this guidance softly pushed aside my own inner compass, so that my thinking, my emotions, my approach to just about anything mimicked their own.

Their approval and validation was the goal, always.

If I had a feeling, a thought, or action, there was a very clear conversation, reaction, or response. Sometimes it was deliberate and conscious: a "No, you're not allowed to do that because . . ." from my mum. Sometimes it was a passing comment and unconscious: a "You never cry; you're fearless" comment from my dad.

They taught me the hustle. That work ethic came before virtually anything else. Mum, a stay-at-home mother, never relaxed. Literally. I never saw her watch TV, read a book, or just sit down and gaze out the window. She was always cooking, cleaning, chauffeuring, volunteering, and financial reconciling. She never stopped. Even at night, she battled insomnia and an overactive, worried mind.

And still, she never stopped.

Dad was one extreme or the other. Working hectic hours in service of clients, you might catch him in his home office at 4 a.m., cracking a key piece of a client dilemma. But on a Saturday—if client work was in the clear—he was living *his* best life. Doing whatever he wanted, whenever he wanted. Serve the client and then serve yourself.

UNPACKING MY UNCONSCIOUS LIMITING BELIEFS

It's interesting to take stock of all these key moments in childhood that stand out to me so clearly; to document these memories and look at them side by side.

The 11-year-old girl on a sugar high from numerous Cokes, getting showered with attention, praise, and affection from one of the most important people in her life over these A letters on the page. Luckily for me at that age, the school system aligned with how I learned. I *was* able to control those grades on the page.

Given my ability to control those grades, and the reaction I received, is it any wonder those letters on the page became synonymous with my self-worth? Is it any wonder I was motivated to continue obsessing and working to achieve those A's? That feedback loop led to engrained study habits, hours poring over textbooks, and a desperate need to achieve to keep my identity intact. In those early years, it all seemed very positive; and it certainly set me on a society-approved-and-celebrated trajectory.

I often wonder, though, what if the school system *hadn't* aligned with my way of learning? What might I have come to believe then? And is it any wonder that I began to associate high productivity—and demonstrable achievement—with worth, identity, and love? And was that a bad thing? Or was it the best start a child could hope for?

Then there were my parents' work lives. My dad's work always served as a sort of trump card. Long hours or client demands gave him full permission to duck out of household and parenting responsibilities on a day-to-day basis. I don't think he ever changed a diaper, cooked us a meal as kids, handled school drop-off and pickup, or did a load of laundry. Why? Because he was busy working. While my mum—the one working within the home—had all the seemingly boring tasks, which never seemed to end. There were always things she had to do for my sister and me; the house could always use tidying; the freezer could always be topped up with meals for the week; there were always people to host. While Dad sat and watched TV, read books, and took naps on his down time, Mum was always on the go doing things that never looked fun.

My observant little mind was unconsciously documenting all of this, of course. Neither of them modelled balance. Dad over-indexed on work outside the home, and Mum over-indexed on work within it. Dad sacrificed deeper relationship and rapport with us as kids. Mum sacrificed her professional pursuits. And so it was that Dad set the standard for what a working life looked like outside the home. His work hours were intense. He was rarely home through the week. I'd learned to respect—and expect—that as a child.

Is it any wonder, then, that as an adult, I would struggle to find balance and fulfillment across all areas of my life? And given that I chose a professional path, is it any wonder that I mimicked my dad's work habits and assumed eighty-hour work weeks were normal? That everything in my life took a back seat to work?

When I sat in the stairwell listening to my parents with their friends and their dinner party conversations, is it any wonder I thought that business and a big, demanding career was the norm? Did thinking that was the norm set me up for business success? Or did it limit my thinking about what earning money could look like, of what a "career" could look like?

As I look at this stack of memories for myself, I can start to unpack them and see how some of my earliest beliefs about work ethic, hustle, productivity, and ambition were shaped. One thing I do know: at a young age, I wasn't thinking through these questions *consciously*. I dare to say that very few of us did as we were growing up.

Our *core limiting beliefs* were influenced by our childhood observations of success, work, and life—what's reasonable and what isn't; what it "should" look like and what it "shouldn't"; what is "good" and "bad." All of these *unconscious limiting beliefs* shaped our entry into the work world and what we want and expect from work—and for our lives.

For me, these *unconscious limiting beliefs* included:

Self-worth is tied to what you produce and how you perform by specific external measures.

Successful people work long hours and make sacrifices in their personal life.

There are good/bad, appropriate/inappropriate, right/wrong ways to earn money.

Always achieve what others set before you.

Fun and rest are not guaranteed; they need to be earned.

There was so much benefit to my upbringing. I know I wouldn't be here today—an independent woman owning and running her own profitable business—without their lessons about work ethic, productivity, and success.

The downside, though, was never establishing a connection to my own inner knowing. I was constantly seeking outside myself for validation and guidance on "the right thing to do." This became habit. And as I grew from a child, to a teenager, to an adult, to a colleague, to a leader, this habit, this pattern, came with me. It was an unconscious pattern that had me continuously looking outside myself, driving to accomplish, complete, and excel at what *others* set before me.

UNPACKING **YOUR** UNCONSCIOUS LIMITING BELIEFS

It can be really challenging to identify, question, and change your core limiting beliefs. And it's one of the reasons why many people come into my coaching practice, although that isn't what they would say. Instead, they share with me that they are feeling "stuck" or "unfulfilled." Their coaching goals might be:

I want to pivot in my career, but it's too late. Now what?
I want more balance in my life. Every time I take a vacation, I spend the entire time on my device.
My friend's net worth is $$$, and I've been in the same role for the last five years.

I want to be a better leader, but I keep getting so frustrated with my team. Nothing I do seems to engage them to drive results.

I have a good job by everyone's standards, yet I'm so unfulfilled. What's wrong with me?

I feel like I'm meant to be doing something more or different, but I have no idea what it is.

I'm so stretched. Is it even possible to have it all? Can I have a great career and be a great parent, a great friend, a great community member, a great coach to my kid's team, and . . .

For each of these issues, there is always a limiting belief or two—or many—operating under the surface that limits their thinking on the situation or how they perceive possibility and opportunity for themselves. That limited thinking translates into actions and behaviors and decisions that leave them feeling blocked, stuck, held back, or unfulfilled.

This is the loop of *unconscious productivity*: goals, ambition, hustle and striving without the inner compass to check in and ask: Is this what I want for *myself*? How am *I* doing? Is how I'm working in service of my life or only in service of others?

Now it's your turn. In your life, where are you feeling stuck, unfulfilled, or in need of change? And what core limiting beliefs might be impacting your behavior? The following worksheet (on page 37) is designed to help you unpack this for yourself.

By working through these beliefs, you are unearthing what's

unconscious and making it *conscious*. By doing this work, you are starting to interrupt the *unconscious productivity* loop and are on your way toward *conscious productivity*!

In the next chapter, we'll explore what happens when our unconscious core beliefs are questioned or challenged by others. Our personality and experience directly influence how we react when this happens. Some might get angry, others might give in, and others might shut down. These reactions—happening quickly and *unconsciously*—can hold you back from your full, authentic expression.

WORKSHEET

IDENTIFY YOUR CORE LIMITING BELIEFS

I'm going to ask you to take a journey back to your childhood, when some of your earliest impressions, beliefs, and experiences about work and productivity began. What you experienced, observed, and got rewarded for shaped the beliefs about work that you now hold as an adult. By unpacking key observations from your childhood, you can identify your unconscious core limiting beliefs.

Using this worksheet, capture five fundamental beliefs about work and life from your childhood. For each belief, answer the questions below:

Fundamental belief	How does this belief impact my behavior?	How does this belief hold me back?	How does this belief serve me?
Belief #1:			
Belief #2:			
Belief #3:			
Belief #4:			
Belief #5:			

You can download the workbook—including all the worksheets, sample worksheets, and bonus reflection questions—at stephaniewoodward.com/resources

CHAPTER 2

YOUR WORK IDENTITY

In the last chapter, we talked about core limiting beliefs and the foundational role they play in shaping your beliefs about work, your relationship with work, and what you believe is possible for you. Next, we're going to explore *personality patterns* and how they relate to your work identity and experience. We all have personality patterns—stemming from both nature and nurture—that contribute to how we are perceived by others and how we show up in the world.

As you go through life, certain things about others—their actions, behaviors, lifestyle—may trigger you. That is, they may elicit a strong, immediate emotional experience for you. This happens so quickly and unconsciously that you'll often react before you even realize that you've been triggered. Too much unconscious reactivity can be at the crux of many challenges in life: unnecessary conflict in relationships, misunderstandings, and hurt feelings. **Your ability to understand your triggers and your impulsive reaction to those triggers can change the course of your professional and personal**

life. I don't say that lightly. I've seen numerous leaders held back from promotion and advancement because of an inability to manage their reactivity. I've seen marriages dissolve because of conflict and misunderstandings based on each individuals' respective triggers and their reactivity to those triggers.

And here's the connection to the work you did in Chapter 1—often, we are triggered when our *unconscious core beliefs* are questioned or challenged. How we then react when triggered is influenced by our personality patterns and lived experience. Some might react with anger, others may acquiesce, while others may withdraw.

Once you are conscious of your core beliefs, understand what triggers you, and how you react, you can move to a place of choice and conscious action. You can start to *consciously* challenge your thought patterns, manage your reactivity, and behave in a different way. **And when your actions, beliefs, and behaviors change, so do your outcomes.**

* * *

There comes a point, typically, where we individuate from our parents. This will happen at a different time for all of us, but for me, it was when I left home for university. University was a given in our household, an expectation. To be honest, as a child, I never knew that ending your education after high school was even a possibility. I was in a very privileged position having this expectation held for me. And while I didn't have that specific explicit word for it at the time—*privilege*—I was aware of this privilege at some level and knew it was something I shouldn't take for granted and shouldn't squander. I felt I had a responsibility of some kind to live into that higher expectation that my family held for me and give it everything I had.

But let me back up for a moment here. What happened to that young woman sitting in that high school English class, the one who loved writing and was also determined to pursue business as a career because, really, was there any other path? A business career and associated life and lifestyle was what my parents knew, and it became what I knew as well. There was no real counseling or discussion of career paths. It was left to us, our parents, perhaps our teachers or other influencers, to research and think about career pathing, which, as a 17-year-old, I didn't even know was a term.

And so, business it was. I pored over university programs and entrance requirements and learned of a very prestigious program that offered early acceptance out of high school. *That*, I decided, was what I was going to do: get pre-accepted to business school. This was no small goal. Competition was stiff. The marks required were high, not to mention the leadership and extracurricular requirements.

I was on the debate club.

I traveled to international speaking competitions.

I was on sports teams: basketball, volleyball, softball.

I was selected for young leader programs.

I ran for student government.

I won English awards and business awards.

I was a volunteer skating coach.

I was a lifeguard and a swimming instructor.

I worked twenty-four hours at the pool every week on top of school and my extracurriculars.

One thing was certain: I was determined. I was going to earn early acceptance to business school, whatever it took. This drive gave me a sense of purpose and meaning. Holding a lofty goal felt incredible, knowing that every day I was making progress against that marker. And it was absolutely something that was within my control. I liked that too.

But there was one major thing missing: joy. And a couple of other things: fun and connection.

Sure, there were glimpses of fun. I went to high school parties; I had plenty of friends. And I *really* loved it when I got a young aspiring swimmer who was terrified of going underwater to relax into it and enjoy it. But I didn't place any value on my own joy or on how much I was laughing or enjoying the journey.

Looking back, it's clear to me that these activities kept me *busy*, which kept me *distracted* from the meaning behind the goal itself. Here I was doing all of these things to land a coveted spot in business school. And yet, I had no idea what "business school" entailed. I was chasing a goal for the goal's sake.

And let me tell you: this worked wonders. Prioritizing educational goals, productivity, and hustle got me so much approval. Accolades. Everyone cheered me on, which then reinforced my "excellent choices" and my work ethic. The praise, validation, and compliments came in and reinforced my drive to succeed and produce above all else.

I was too busy for any inward focus. I did not have a spare minute to do or think about anything outside of my one-track goal: get pre-accepted to business school.

And so it was my Grade 13 year and I was sitting at home in our sunroom, which was living up to its name on that June afternoon: the floor-to-ceiling curtainless windows gave free pass to every ray of sun. The whir of the air conditioner approached a hiss, indignant that it had landed this particular lot to cool.

In front of me on the dining room table was the acceptance letter. I'd done it.

Despite the liter of water I had just knocked back, my mouth remained dry. I lifted the cherry popsicle from the bowl beside me and bit off the tip, the freeze zinged its way through my front teeth and gave me something to focus on rather than the letter.

I'd landed the holy grail of that year's aspiring business major graduates: pre-acceptance to one of the most highly coveted business school spots. Guaranteed. I could study anything and keep my spot, the letter stated, on two conditions: that I maintained a set GPA overall and a 70 percent average in one of the prerequisite business course. Easy-peasy.

I'd been working toward this exact outcome for all five years of high school. And I'd done it.

Mum and Dad were thrilled. Ecstatic was more like it. The news was announced at every dinner party and each meeting Dad attended. Cards of congratulations arrived in the mail. It was a big deal. People were impressed. I was officially *going places*. I still wasn't sure what those *places* were other than a vague notion of business consulting.

But I was a big deal in everyone's eyes. I even allowed myself to exhale. It felt like I had found my place in the world. There was a determined path in front of me. One that provided a clear path to that world of business I'd witnessed and aspired to since sitting on the fourth step, peering through the bannisters.

This was the plan. It had always been the plan, hadn't it? Sitting at the bar, going over my report card grades, the plan had been made: I'd study business and go on to be a management consultant. Dad was a management consultant, and all of his smart, fun, and well-dressed friends were management consultants. I'd won the Business Award at graduation. This was my path. Everyone knew this was my path. My pen hovered over the page. It was time to check the "accept" box.

I chomped down on the rest of the cherry popsicle, my brain zinging and freezing as I placed the check mark of acceptance on the page.

* * *

Ambition, fear, and insecurity hung in the air like a fog in the business school classroom. We were all second year university students and this particular class was the gateway to business school. I was one of two students who had been pre-accepted to the program—as long as I earned a 70 percent in this prerequisite class. Which, of course, would happen. It was less a sense of cockiness I felt and more of a self-trust, knowing my commitment and work ethic. I'd succeed because I gave myself no other option. I'd sit in the library and at my desk, for as many hours as it took for the learning to sink in and the assignments to be completed. Full stop.

I'd wanted to keep my status hidden and would have been happy to hide quietly in the class, scribbling notes. But there was no hiding in this classroom: the room was set up with giant semicircular tables, stadium seating style, so that all of us could see one another and the teacher at all times. Truth be told, nobody wanted to be hidden. It was a class to be seen and noticed in, to stand out and earn the endorsement of the professor: a short, stout woman with tight gray curls, pursed lips, and steely-green eyes that pierced through glasses that were too big for her face.

"We have two pre-accepted students," she declared on the first day of class, her tone almost one of taunting, as she pointed out Jeremy and me. Or was I imagining it? All eyes on all levels looked upon us in that moment, as we both looked at each another. Our fellow classmates looked at us with either awe or resentment, or a mixture of both. We had what all of them wanted. The sentiment in the room became very clear very quickly: they expected Jeremy and me to be the classroom whiz kids or to crack under the pressure and lose our spot to free it up for one of them. The professor continued, "As for the rest of you, let the race begin."

Seats were assigned; mine was front row just to the right of the teacher. Each of us had an electrical outlet for our laptop computers, which was mega high tech and rare in the late '90s. Even the chairs were plush faux leather, designed to give us a taste of corporate life.

There was something disconcerting to me as I looked around the room of 20-year-olds in their suits, pulling laptops from briefcases. All little mini-me's of corporate fathers, mothers, or whoever happened to be their *Forbes* business icon. It was like a giant game of dress-up.

We had two classes per week. One to introduce the selected business case for the week and the second to discuss our analysis as a class. Pages of business equations and formulas would help us in this analysis: predictors of financial health, supply chain efficiency, and cash flow analysis. There was something about those equations that didn't sit well with me. I'd always had an aptitude for math and the calculations were straightforward and simple. It was nothing compared to the math acrobatics of algebra and geometry in high school. Yet despite their simplicity, I simply couldn't get excited about calculating inventory turnover and supply chain costs.

The interpersonal dynamics of the case, though, fascinated me. Poring over this week's case in my room that night, it struck me that the business in question had a very inexperienced leader. I wondered if his decisions were being dictated by a desire to appear decisive and action-oriented, to essentially prove himself, instead of what was right for the business. There seemed to be a bravado behind some of his actions. As I continued through the case, I was struck by what seemed to be reactive, knee-jerk decisions. But none of the equations pointed to an issue.

My hand shot up in class for the group analysis that week, as I described my concern.

"Leadership is an intangible, Stephanie. You should know that."

The professor lifted her chin and tugged the lapel of her jacket in tighter as she peered down at me. "This is why we look at the numbers. Remember: *Objectivity*."

"But surely future profitability and sustainability is impacted by a leader's ability—" I continued.

"Intangible!" She cut in, chopping my sentence in the air. She raised a pointed finger and aimed it across the classroom. "Jeremy, take us through your analysis." And just like that, I was silenced, and Jeremy continued the case analysis.

Someone behind me snickered, "Maybe you're destined for Human Remains." Human Remains was the term classmates had started using for Human Resources, which was considered business for those who couldn't make it in "real" business roles. It was the unruly, non-serious business family member that executives were forced to contend with.

Objectivity—and financial analysis—was key, the professor emphasized, because it could be measured, tracked, and proven. Intangibles were their own special category.

Intangibles.

As I walked home from class that afternoon, I thought about my philosophy and psychology classes and the political leaders who had wreaked havoc through history. It was their beliefs and their leadership approach that led to some of the most horrendous outcomes in history, not necessarily their objective economic policies or how they accounted for the depreciation of assets. We were a world made up of people. Where was the humanness in the financial analysis? Where were the people?

I was fired up.

Intangible. The word rolled around in my head as I went back over the case that night. Leadership, engagement, interpersonal dynamics. Surely those must impact business. I read about patents and good-will and intellectual property. These were the acceptable, somewhat quantifiable, intangibles. There were rules about how they could be measured and presented on the balance sheet. But leadership, and people, were nowhere to be found in the equations. Other than as a salary and total compensation expense on the income statement. An expense to be managed and handled.

As I trudged my way through the tangibles—machinery, inventory, office furniture amortization—I felt my eyelids droop.

I stopped by the professor's office hours that week, pronouncing my objections to the system and how we were expected to analyze the cases for class. She pulled her glasses from her eyes and rested them on the desk in front of her. A deep red ridge remained where the bottom frame of the glasses had sat. "The system isn't perfect, Stephanie," she quipped, pulling together a haphazardly stacked pile of papers in her hands and tapping them into aligned submission. "But it's what we've got."

I felt my eyes on hers, imploring her to say more. "And it's what you'll be evaluated on in class!" she added, resolute and forceful, as she broke the silence between us.

I couldn't shake it. The case analysis. The teacher. I hated this class.

I don't want to study this, a voice in my head began whispering to me in the evenings as I worked my way through yet another business case.

The words jumped around me as I lay bug-eyed in bed. What other choice did I have? If business wasn't my path, what was? What was wrong with me that I didn't want this coveted spot? And I rolled about with those questions, entangling the sheets as I flipped and flopped.

LESSONS IN LEADERSHIP

It's so interesting to me how times have changed since I sat in that business school classroom. Perhaps my experience was entirely due to one particular professor's preferences. Thankfully, leadership and people strategy are now considered critical determinants of business success and competitiveness, and they form a core part of business school programs. But back in the day, in that class, the emphasis was on financial calculation. I often wonder what might have happened if I'd sat in a different class or checked my assumptions about what I thought I was learning in that course. This one experience left such a sour taste in my mouth and led to a series of life-changing decisions.

It also ignited my passion for leadership—both formal and informal—and its impact in the workplace.

Leadership styles significantly influence both outcomes and the workplace culture. Culture is set at the top, so the leadership styles of those in positions of power across the workplace not only dictate *what* gets done, but *how* it gets done. A leader who leads and reacts *unconsciously* is going to create a very different workplace experience compared to a leader who leads and responds *consciously*. The leader's approach then impacts the interpersonal and team dynamics within the organization as a whole.

It's why human leadership and team dynamics in the workplace fascinate me. Work provides a perfect environment to call you out on all of your firmly held core beliefs: about yourself, about work, about productivity, about worth. At work, you come face to face with a (hopefully) diverse group of people that you haven't necessarily chosen and have to work with under pressure and stress—as they push up against your core beliefs, and you push up against theirs. Your ability and skill to navigate these dynamics *consciously* can transform your workplace experience.

Consider the leader who has an *unconscious limiting belief* that in order to be successful, one must always power through regardless of circumstances. Now imagine they have someone on their team who does not hold the same belief. This individual has a bad cold, and takes a day off in the midst of a big project. Since the leader is *unconscious* to their own limiting belief, they have a harsh reaction. They now perceive this individual on their team as less committed, less ambitious, and less viable for promotion.

When I share this example with clients individually or in workshops, I hear a lot of backlash:

"But it's important to have a work ethic!"
"Wouldn't we all like to just call in sick or take a mental health day when things get hard! But it's important to be responsible."
"This younger generation just doesn't work as hard as we did."

These reactions typically come from individuals who share a similar limiting belief to the leader in the example.

Now let's consider the response of a leader *with the same limiting belief*, but who is *conscious of it*. Their train of thought may go something like this:

I know it's a trigger for me when a person takes a sick day in the midst of a project.

I certainly don't show myself any compassion when I'm sick—I tough it out.

But that's not necessarily the best way to handle sickness.

Sumara has been doing good work on this project up until now. The issue isn't really that she's off sick—the issue is that I'm concerned about the impact on the project timelines. This is a highly visible project and I'm stressed about that.

I'll check in with her quickly to see how she's doing and make sure we're on track with the project deadlines.

She knows she's responsible for these deadlines, and I trust she'll rework her plan, as needed, to meet them.

Notice the difference between an *unconscious reaction* and a *conscious response*. In this example, the conscious leader was able to separate their different beliefs about sick days from the underlying issue: the project timelines. Her response doesn't shame or diminish Sumara for her different perspective about taking a sick day. Instead, the response honors both their different beliefs about work *and* the business outcomes.

Which leader would you rather be? And which leader would you rather follow?

How you consistently show up at work forms your work identity— how you're perceived by your peers and whether you are trusted and respected by them as well. When you show up at work *unconscious* of your limiting beliefs, you are at the mercy of whatever might trigger you on a particular day and your unconscious reaction to that trigger. Getting *conscious* about your limiting beliefs—and how they impact your work identity—makes it easier for you to pause when you are triggered. That pause gives you the chance to manage your reactivity and choose your response. Coming from a conscious response will almost always produce better outcomes.

* * *

That weekend, I wanted nothing to do with my oversized oak desk or the sixteen-page unfinished business case spread across it. I wanted to run away to my childhood home and my mum's chicken casserole.

It was my first experience with the overwhelmingly, immediately gratifying bliss of denial and escape. If I don't attend business class, does it really exist? If I just ignore it, maybe it will go away.

The truth was, no, it would not go away. Failing to show up for class was a serious offense. Two absences could result in losing my guaranteed spot in business school for the following year. That was fact. The business school ice I'd been treading on for the school year was no longer thin; it was cracking. I didn't buy what business school was selling. My rebellion for the course teachings had led me to submit a case the previous week with minimal financial analysis of the traditional sense and a deep analysis of the psychological threats I saw for the company. It earned me a failing grade. I was at risk of falling under the 70 percent grade requirement.

I could fail this course.

The thought rippled through me as I stuffed a weekend's worth of clothes and my toothbrush in a bag, and I felt my body seize with dread. If I pushed the panic aside, though, there was a single sentence floating in the background that whispered: *then you'll never need to analyze supply chain process again.* The panic was quick to override it, though: *it also means you'll be a big fucking failure.*

It was the panic that rode shotgun with me for the two-hour drive home. I stepped through the back door, dropped my bags, and breathed in the mix of herbs and spices wafting from the kitchen. The air felt humid and heavy and held the dinner scents like a warm blanket as it wrapped around me.

In our family kitchen, there was a ledge—more of a nook, really—in front of the microwave, between the fridge and the pantry. This nook between the fridge and the pantry and above and below the cabinets is where my five foot eight frame scrunched, knees bunched up tight to my chest, back pressed up against the side of the pantry, toes curled up and white as they pushed against the side of the fridge. It was an upright fetal position. The ledge itself wasn't deep, maybe a foot and a half. And it wasn't wide either. But it held my scrunched-up frame perfectly. My head curled in, ear resting on my knee, and I gazed out sideways at the kitchen.

In this space, I felt safe. Mum was on the other side of the kitchen island stirring something at the stove, and beyond her, the sunroom was lit by the late afternoon light streaming in through the windows. Outside, the leaves were coming to life in their full color glory, unapologetic attention seekers as they burst through the spring air. The bamboo blinds cut the vista every few centimeters, so the lime green of the leaves peeked through the cracks, and the remaining sunlight poured in where it could, casting stripes across the kitchen. I uncurled my hand and stretched it out sideways to catch one of the stripes, letting it draw a diagonal from my pinky to my thumb. A tear dropped to my shoulder as my gaze steadied on the warm, sunny band. Moving my arm forward, I watched the stripe work its way across my wrist and on to my forearm. I hadn't mentioned a word of my business class issues to my parents.

I am a train wreck. A failure. I felt the tears brimming. *I need to tell her.*

It felt as though my entire life—past, present, and future—was being held in that moment, on that ledge, in that stripe, in those tears. Years of assumed ambition, of striving, of expectations, and firmly held beliefs crumbled in my mind. My life, as it had been planned, was falling apart. And I had no idea what it meant.

I'd walked through the door only fifteen minutes ago, having had the drive home to twist and turn the decision points in my mind, considering each and every windy permutation. There was still no clear end point, only one immediate choice.

Perching in this ledge was my return-home habit. I'd catch up with Mum as she finished dinner, as she was doing that night. In her world, nothing was out of the ordinary. Whereas in mine, everything was.

"Mum?"

She didn't turn around, just continued stirring, with an "Mm-hmm" slipping from her lips as she brought the wooden spoon to her mouth and tasted the soup.

I'm not going to business school next year.
I hate financial reports.
I hate investment theory.
I think the system is broken.
I'm changing my major.

Instead of speaking any of those words, I just started crying. Mum put the spoon down on the counter and hurried over. My head was now buried in my knees, and I felt her hand on my back. I rarely ever cried. "Stephie . . . what is it?" The softness in her voice brought on more tears.

"I . . . I can't go to . . . business school."

There. The words were spoken. The years of straight A's. The pre-acceptance. All for nothing.

* * *

I could still feel the path the tears had taken across my face, their salty tracks drying on my skin as I went into my bedroom, closed the door and folded onto the bed.

What now?

I wasn't going to business school. Mum had listened to me, asked a few questions, and had then just let the decision sit in the air between us. No yelling, no second-guessing, but no affirmation either. I breathed in deeply. I felt lighter in some ways, the fear of speaking the decision now behind me. But that fear void was quickly filling with something new: the uncertainty of what came next. If I wasn't a business major, with pre-acceptance to an elite program, who was I? Was I no longer to become a management consultant? If someone asked me what I was going to do after graduation, what was my answer now?

I pulled my pillow in and over my head, scrunching it around my face and ears, hoping to suffocate the words running rampant in my mind. It wasn't enough, though, to drown out the sound of Dad coming home from work. I heard the familiar thump of the briefcase being tossed against the laundry wall, the clank of his keys landing on the kitchen island, and the definitive clack of his dress shoes against the Mexican tiles as he crossed the kitchen.

I froze on the bed. He was going to be furious. How would I tell him? I imagined him screaming that I was wasting my talent and throwing my life away. The scene then switched to him hunched over the basement bar, shaking his head in disappointment, telling me there was nothing left to say. I imagined my outrage, my protests, my words of retort.

His footsteps traveled up the stairs, and I could hear him on the other side of my bedroom door. If he came in, he'd see the red puffiness of my face, he'd know something was up. I braced myself for the knock on the door. It didn't come. Instead, I heard him pass by and head into my parents' bedroom. The sound of running water; the closet door opening; the squeak of the bedroom door opening and closing again. And then the padding of his feet as he went back down the stairs.

It was only when I exhaled that I realized I'd been holding my breath the entire time.

Mum will tell him.

I imagined them sitting at the bar now together, as Mum shared my announcement. Dad with a scotch in hand and Mum with a gin and tonic. In the movie of my mind, the clink of ice cubes shattered my dad's seething rage as he prepared himself to storm up the stairs and burst into my bedroom. How would I defend my decision? As my stomach churned, ready for the attack, I planned my arguments. But I felt the tears creep back up at the thought of his disappointment and anger.

But Dad never came upstairs. I fell asleep at some point and awoke in the middle of the night, fully clothed in a fetal position with the pillow perched across my right ear. It was 3 a.m. The house was silent; all the lights were out. Mum and Dad had gone to bed. My sister had either come home quietly or stayed at a friend's.

I tossed and turned for the rest of the night, catching sleep in twenty-five-minute bursts, questioning what the morning would bring. As the light poked through the blinds, I heard the shuffling of movement and spoons brushing up against coffee cups being stirred. This is it. The moment of reckoning. I pulled on a well-worn sweatshirt lying next to the bed and sauntered downstairs.

I was greeted by Mum as she wiped down the kitchen island and reached for her keys. She was headed to the grocery store and would then be meeting Dad at the golf club for a late afternoon round. He was already there, she explained, to get a quick round in before the course got too busy.

Did you tell him?
Is he mad?
What did he say?
Why didn't he come and see me last night?

These were all the questions I wanted to ask—but didn't. And my mum didn't volunteer any information.

When I arrived back at school that night, I sat on my single bed and flipped through the course calendar and offerings, bypassing the entire business section. I had no real direction in mind. Yet I'd never felt more clear, more sure. Even the air felt clearer, the stifle of judgment nowhere to be found. And if I was being honest and allowed myself to mark the sentiment before the slap of guilt knocked it from my mind, for the first time in my life, I was happy to be hours away from home.

Dad never spoke to me about that decision. In fact, I don't remember him speaking to me much for the rest of that year.

* * *

It was psychology that stole my intellectual heart for the next two years. I felt like I'd finally found the information and answers I'd been seeking. Theories around personalities and how our environment played a significant role in who we'd become. I'd sit in class, in the front row, engrossed, and spend the night reading supplemental material. Here was where the intangibles of business and life came alive. I wanted to burst back through the business school doors and overlay everything I'd learned against every single business case.

Sadly, not everyone held psychology in the same esteem as I did. Over a year later, my dad was still barely speaking to me. He'd actually never confronted me about the decision. Or talked it through with me. Or even acknowledged the decision. When guests came to the house over the summer and asked me about my major and plans and how school was going, he'd leave the room as I shared my new path.

Those guests in the house gave me the look I'd expected from Dad: disappointment, confusion, and sometimes outrage. "Psychology? Really? Weren't you pre-accepted to business?"

Opinions were served up without reservation; everyone was forthcoming in their disbelief and disagreement with my decision. There was no prestige in announcing an Honors Psychology degree. And yet, I felt I had learned more about the world, human kind, and business through studying psychology for two years than I had in a lifetime's worth of math classes, business classes, and theory.

But the job market didn't mirror my enthusiasm. There was no

"Chief Psychology Officer" position at any company, and not a single job description asked for a psychology degree. And with my dramatic career path shift, I'd lost all of my mentors. No one was standing by ready to advise me on my career options now. I pored over graduate school programs, took the GREs, and completed aptitude tests for clues. And then, there it was. The article that changed it all for me spoke of corporate communications and how important it was for businesses to connect with their "stakeholders." This was a new word for me; I'd never heard anything about business stakeholders or why they were important to keep in mind. But I was immediately hooked. Writing, people, and business. All together in one role.

Sign me up.

I soon discovered a graduate program at Boston University, specializing specifically in corporate public relations. Applications were due eight weeks from that day. The countdown was on and the goal was clear: I was on my way to graduate school in the US. I had found my place in business.

Boston University—and my two years in Boston—were some of the happiest of my life. I'd returned to Canada after graduation, and as far as I knew, I was the only one in Toronto—possibly even the country—with this particular degree. And my soul sang as I worked my way through business cases about connecting with stakeholders, managing crises, and community outreach programs. In those classes, I felt I had found my career home. Dad, too, was beaming with pride at my graduation. I was the first in my family to earn a master's degree, and the degree would lead me back to the corporate world. The world he knew and could advise me on. And Mum was thrilled to see me incorporate writing and communication into my career path. She knew better than I did at that point that putting words to paper and connecting with people is what brought me to life.

I'd done it. I made both of them happy, while also making myself happy. But looking back now on that 23-year-old version of myself, I know one thing to be true: I was happier that they were happy; happier that I'd been accepted and that Dad had celebrated this path. It was still them—my external validators—driving my life.

The decision to not go to business school was my first experience of tuning inward and listening to myself and what I TRULY wanted, not because it was easy (telling everyone was one of the hardest things I've ever done) and not because it was comfortable (business school was *the thing* that all my hard work, ambition, and hustle had been in service of. I'd had it all figured out and I was *so close* to executing on the plan that I thought was my path). It was that within me, deep down, it felt *right*. As soon as I made that decision, there was a feeling of lift, of lightness, like a weight being removed from my heart and from my soul.

THE ENNEAGRAM

I remember feeling so relieved when I discovered that program at Boston University. Yes, I was excited about the program. But equally exciting? The fact that I'd found a way to earn my parents' approval and validation again—especially my dad's. I was still very caught up in the loop of *unconscious productivity*—setting goals and hustling in ways that would earn me external approval. Of course, I didn't know that, then.

A personal development journey sure can feel like a slog sometimes. It can take a lifetime to unpack all of your core beliefs and personality patterns. And in my work as a coach, my clients aren't willing to wait a lifetime for changes and results.

Is there a way to accelerate the process? I'm not talking about "hacking" your way through this work. Changing behaviors will always take effort and work on your part, and it won't always feel easy or comfortable (in fact, it often won't). However, through my experience—and I've tested *a lot* of tools, techniques, and personality assessments—I have found one tool that I believe is transformational for this work and can accelerate your self-awareness journey both personally and professionally.

This tool is the Enneagram, which provides powerful insight that can be applied across all areas of your life. It outlines nine personality archetypes and provides a map for personal growth for each of those types. Here, I will give you a high-level introduction to the nine personality types (and what they over-focus on) for the purpose of your own self-awareness journey, to help you start to identify and deepen your understanding of your own personality patterns.

The type descriptions are based on the teachings of CP Enneagram Academy, led by Beatrice Chestnut and Uranio Paes.

ENNEAGRAM CORE TYPES

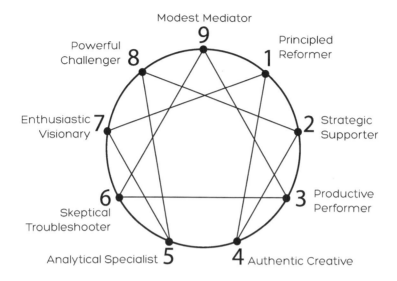

Note: Core type names vary. The above is based on the teachings of CP Enneagram Academy.

For more information on the Enneagram core types, visit stephaniewoodward.com/resources to download the workbook and supplementary materials.

ENNEAGRAM CORE TYPES: AREAS OF OVER-FOCUS

Enneagram 1: Principled Reformer

They tend to over-focus on: what needs to be fixed; mistakes, errors; what's the "right" way; how to avoid showing their flaws; keeping up ideal or perfect standards; what's right/wrong, good/bad.

Enneagram 2: Strategic Supporter

They tend to over focus on: what other (important) people want; connection; what's going on in their relationships; being liked, admired, and wanted; opportunities to be influential.

Enneagram 3: Productive Performer

They tend to over focus on: being the one to make things happen; being central; taking refuge in getting things done; projecting a good image (proving "goodness" and competence); competing to win; outrunning their feelings.

Enneagram 4: Authentic Creative

They tend to over focus on: what's going on in their internal world; big feelings; how they stack up to others (feeling "less than"); what's missing in their lives; desire to feel special.

Enneagram 5: Analytical Specialist

They tend to over focus on: how to conserve their energy; external expectations, demands, and needs (and wanting to avoid those external expectations); controlling their time.

Enneagram 6: Skeptical Troubleshooter

They tend to over focus on: detecting and scanning for threats; looking for good authority, allies; skill and readiness in the face of attack; neutralizing and solving problems; things that signal danger and/or problems.

Enneagram 7: Enthusiastic Visionary

They tend to over focus on: mental stimulation, imagination, constantly making associations between things; looking to the future, planning; escaping limitations; seeking interesting experiences (variety, novelty).

Enneagram 8: Powerful Challenger

They tend to over focus on: the big picture—and how they can impact the situation; asserting territory; power and strength to impact things the way they want to; measuring up the strengths and weaknesses of others; who to protect/take care of.

Enneagram 9: Modest Mediator

They tend to over focus on: external needs and demands over their own ("self-forgetting"), creating harmony over tension (how to "fix" the tension) and the outward environment (rather than on their internal environment).

I'm an Enneagram Type 9. If you look at the description, you'll see that as the *modest mediator*, I seek harmony and am adept at perspective taking (sometimes to my detriment). The challenge for my personality archetype is *self-forgetting*. Meaning, I lose sight of my *own* perspectives, opinions, needs, and wants. Bringing this piece of information into my *conscious* awareness—that my personality predisposes me to self-forget and overly value others' perspectives—immediately accelerated my personal growth process.

Once I learned this about myself, I couldn't unlearn it. The Enneagram helped me to see those patterns for what they were: *patterns*, rather than fixed ways of thinking, feeling, and behaving. And patterns are changeable—if we're willing to put in the work.

What I love most about the Enneagram is that it is a system for personal evolution. Many personality profiling tools will assign you to a category, type, or profile, then provide strategies for working *around* that profile. The Enneagram, on the other hand, provides a system to help you to move *past* the limitations of your personality patterns so that, over time, you are breaking through limiting behavior patterns and raising your level of consciousness.

Think of those times you've been in a meeting and thought to yourself: *I just don't understand where they're coming from!* Or *why can't they seem to understand the issue with this?* From an Enneagram perspective, we will all perceive a situation differently and react differently, depending on our Enneagram type. Each type sees the world through their particular lens. Once you recognize that it is a lens, you are free to remove the lens and experience the world differently. This is why I find the Enneagram so transformational—it gives you the tools to move from *unconscious beliefs and personality patterns* to *conscious* consideration and deliberate action almost immediately.

Even taking a quick scan at the nine core types on page 63—and what they focus on—imagine family and workplace dynamics and how they might be influenced by the interactions and predispositions of the different types. Imagine what natural affinities might arise between types and the natural conflict that may arise between others.

Knowing what I know about the Enneagram, I often sit back and think about the interplay of the nine personality types in a workplace and how interesting it is:

- Some come in believing that work is core to their identity and self-worth.
- Some come in thinking results are what matter most; whereas others place relationships before outcomes.
- Some have a very fixed perspective on what's right and wrong.
- Some see risk and worst-case scenarios, where others see only opportunity.
- Some come in risk averse; others, risk seeking.
- Some love routine; some love novelty.
- Some seek harmony; others love to stir the pot.
- Some are direct in their delivery, while others soften their statements.
- Some like to analyze quietly; some like to talk it out.

Then overlay limiting beliefs from childhood. All that programming and all of those beliefs that were formed in our early years—along with our personality patterns—get brought into the workplace with us and form our expectations . . .

- About what work should be and look like.
- How we should work.
- How others should work.
- What constitutes "good" work habits and "bad."
- How we react when others don't see things "our" way.

This last point is a critical one. It influences how we perceive and react to others. It's no wonder, then, that work can be a place of conflict and stress OR a place of joy and fulfillment—depending on how every person's beliefs and patterns play out in the workplace.

We see a job ad, have a few conversations, and BOOM, we're placed in an ecosystem of pressure, stretch goals, and expectations with a group of other humans who may have very different beliefs, conditioning, and expectations from our own. And we'll be spending forty to one hundred hours a week with this group of humans, working on this list of things, working toward these specific timeframes.

Eventually, choices will be made about who gets promoted, who become leaders. You may be put in charge and take on the responsibility for leading others through this environment, or you may not. You'll find yourself reporting in to a leader—perhaps a series of leaders over the span of your career—who may or may not have the same beliefs, conditioning, and expectations about work as you. And they now determine your career future, and they evaluate how you go about doing your work.

When we can show up conscious of our limiting beliefs and personality patterns, the work experience improves for everyone.

I only wish I'd been conscious of my own limiting beliefs and Enneagram Type 9 predisposition to self-forget when I entered the workforce all those years ago.

* * *

I took all my zeal, ambition, and work ethic, and I naively entered the workforce with unbridled enthusiasm and a determined spirit. I was ready to be given a chance—any chance—to demonstrate my value. And I was determined to do an excellent—check that: *perfect*—job.

What was your first workspace? A cubicle, office, family-style table, or "pen"? Mine was a cubicle, shortly followed by a converted supply closet office. I came into that cubicle and supply closet office bright-eyed, my brain full of classroom theory, cases, and project work. Despite the conversations and discussions about ethics in the classroom, nothing truly prepared me for the first time I faced pressure as a corporate communicator to "spin" the truth—or twist it into a barely truthful narrative. I heard people refer to me as a spin doctor when I shared my title, and over time, I came to understand how this moniker originated. I also met and witnessed individuals and organizations doing phenomenal work, who were truly seeking input from key stakeholders and communicating with integrity and vision in a really practical, lived experience kind of way that no classroom case study could capture. Those were the organizations I chose to work for.

And there were all the people I met: my new colleagues, coworkers, and kitchen coffee-making companions.

My dad, of course, was thrilled as I stepped into the corporate life he'd always dreamed of for me. I would design strategy, present to committees, boards, and manage people, projects, and teams. The champagne was popped, steaks made their way to the grill, and our family Sunday night dinner was filled with a celebratory cheer.

"Here's to the working girl!" he toasted, raising his glass well above his head. All four family arms reached in across the table and clinked in agreement.

Despite my dad's enthusiastic congratulations and the warm welcome at the workplace, I felt an ongoing surge of stress in those early days. I had this intense desire to understand and please this new really important person in my life, my boss. "Boss" had become the new critical authority, the new external validator in my life. Up until now, it had been parents, teachers, and friends. "Boss" was new, and I didn't know the rules. But I figured I had to learn them fast and perform.

I was the first to arrive at the office, giant to-go coffee in hand, and the last staff member to turn off her office lights at night. I'd dream about work, often coming up with my best ideas in the wee hours of the night. I'd email myself my musings and ramblings from bed and pick them back up once I'd surfaced and returned to my desk in the morning.

I was everything my boss had hoped for: dedicated, smart, hard-working, and—though he absolutely never said it explicitly—single, and making no real effort to change that status. Meaning I could work late and on weekends, with no other claims on my time or attention. My singledom certainly contributed to my success in my twenties. I watched, without full appreciation or understanding, my female colleagues balance work demands, marriages, and newborns. While they grappled about when to return from maternity leave, there was nothing holding me back from powering through and soldiering on. That was its own sacrifice, of course, as I had very little life to speak of outside of work. But from a career perspective, it was ideal.

I witnessed many up-and-coming managers and executives grapple with what I now know to be really challenging—often heartbreaking—decisions. Choosing between career progression and time with their kids. While this most often fell on my female colleagues, I also saw brutal sexism directed at men who chose to take paternity leave or those who partnered on the parenting responsibilities. One thing was clear: those who weren't available at all times weren't getting ahead nearly as quickly as those who were. Full stop.

And so the new rules were quickly becoming clear: availability and results were the currency in this new world.

Because full-time relationship, marriage, and children were nowhere near my radar, I was able to follow these rules well. I was the go-to for every project, the right hand to the executives. And so I worked. And worked. I worked to the point that I forgot—simply by absence—how empty my bachelor apartment actually was.

The executives were all besotted. *You'll go far*, they all promised. *We'll set you up for success.*

* * *

A year in, I was on top of the world. I was at all the senior leadership meetings, trusted and asked to advise on all the top issues. Some tried to start rumors that I must be having an affair with one of the executives to be so successful so young. But the informal influencers of the office put a stop to those rumors pretty quickly: "Stephanie dresses way too conservatively to be having an affair."

Yep. THAT's what saved me from the rumors. Not my track record or my endless hours working or the fact that there was no rationale or evidence for these rumors. It was my wardrobe. My don't-notice-me-but-see-me-as-professional gray and black pantsuits kept me from being the subject of gossip, ridicule, and rumor as I worked eighty hours a week.

And so entered another rule: dress to avoid any form of controversy. All of it reinforced this need for a perfect persona, perfect costume, in order to stay safe and respected. I was one red-painted nail or too-revealing hemline away from losing everyone's respect.

And so I put on the uniform, every single day. I watched what I said. I crafted my responses. I prepared for *everything*.

I was promoted quickly, higher and higher up the ladder, up the chain of command.

Status meetings and performance reviews became the report cards of adulthood. Hours worked, the new measure of success. I very quickly became the model employee. The one others were expected to compare themselves against. Every word I uttered was monitored, assessed as I became the standard. And so perfection became my only comparator. I planned and questioned every article of clothing: too subdued? Too showy? Every interaction: too distant? Too familiar? It all needed to be thought through, planned, and executed with precision and a smile.

The work needed to get done. And the workload never ceased. There was always another issue to fix, system to improve, or process to modernize.

Night after night, I found myself collapsing on the couch, with the days' happenings whirring through my mind. My phone buzzed at all hours, every day of the week. Mostly it was my boss, sometimes other colleagues. And so a habit began of taking my computer to the couch and settling into an evening of work.

* * *

There was a common theme throughout my earlier career: I was young and inexperienced to have the responsibility I held. This wasn't lost on me, nor was I able to forget or ignore it. I had direct reports that were significantly older than me—sometimes fifteen to twenty years older—often people who wanted the exact position I held. I took this seriously and was hyper-aware of my "inexperience," which led to two things: (1) an even greater level of preparation for everything I did, and (2) I was introduced to yet more external validators: *the colleague* and *the direct report*. I had entirely new categories of people I needed to please.

I knew it would be incredibly important to earn respect and credibility within this team, with "earn" being the key word because my résumé could never be extensive enough, my past successes never stellar enough to appease everybody. This led to a fascination with leadership—leadership effectiveness, leadership optimization, emotional intelligence, and interpersonal dynamics. If there was a topic related to leadership, I was studying it, learning it, and making myself put it into practice.

I found myself drawing on my love of psychology and people in general. I paid attention to the dynamics between the individuals on my team and to the dynamics within other departments of the organization. I could sense power struggles, insecurity, arrogance, and empathy in others. And so I adjusted my approach and style when sensing a power struggle or an insecurity. I observed the dynamics in the room before a meeting started so that I kept them in mind as I facilitated the discussion.

From my studies and late-night reading, as well as observing other leaders around me at the office, I quickly learned a few things: good leadership was directly connected to self-awareness and personal development. You had to work on yourself and be aware of your own strengths, limitations, and beliefs before you could effectively lead others. And years of experience in no way equated to effective leadership. Conscious effort and attention were the key.

My ongoing efforts at self-awareness and personal growth and development led to incessant, ongoing chatter in my mind:

Is it appropriate for me to speak up right now?

Is it my place?

Had I created opportunities for everyone to speak?

Was I dominating the conversation?

Was I withdrawing?

Had I provided enough context?

How was this landing with the team?

Will my speaking undermine someone else at the table?

Might someone's power feel threatened?

How would my opinion or recommendation affect the others
around this table?

Was I pushing an agenda?

I adjusted the way I spoke and delivered my messages, depending on the group, the dynamics, and my relative power. It was exhausting. And not everyone was doing it. I had executives who tried to talk me out of it, saying I was being too soft or not moving things forward fast enough, and that not everyone's input mattered.

There were so many conflicting opinions—and from those external validators who I now cared so much about: Board members, senior executives, boss, colleagues, and direct reports. I had to balance what I was reading and learning about in all those books with how I was being evaluated, with my lived experience with my teams, and all the while trying to honor my values and stay in integrity. Over time, my leadership ratings came in strong, morale on my team was strong, and my results were strong. And so I persevered.

As I entered the workforce, I became even further enmeshed with *unconscious productivity*. Parents and teachers were swapped out for executives, bosses, and colleagues as external validators and comparators. Organizational goals were set for me—and I continued my pattern of achieving goals for the goal's sake.

The one caveat being: How does the goal impact my team? My Enneagram Type 9 personality was in full effect—considering the perspectives of, and impacts to, everyone around me. Those executives who tried to talk me out of it, saying I was being too soft and that not everyone's input mattered? Definitely not Type 9s! They were bringing their personality lens and perspective to bear on the situation, as was I, and yet because we were all operating *unconsciously*, these differences of opinion felt like irreconcilable differences, rather than simply different lenses through which to view a particular issue, which led each of us to "over focus" on something different. Because I wasn't aware of the Enneagram personality lenses at the time, I didn't have language to navigate those situations.

Instead, I felt constantly torn between pleasing these new external validators and what I felt was right for my team. It was only when I received *external measures*—high leadership ratings, engagement scores, and team morale—that I started to trust my approach to leadership.

Had the other executives and I had the insight of the Enneagram at that time—we would have been *conscious* of our personality lenses and could have respected one another's personality *strengths* and owned our areas of over-focus in navigating the day-to-day departmental issues. In this way, the Enneagram is a tool that can shift the way you experience work.

This is why personal development work—and deepening your self-awareness—is so critical to *conscious productivity*: so that you show up in the workplace (and the other areas of your life) *consciously*—with an understanding of your limiting beliefs and your particular personality lens; knowing it is just that—*a lens*. When realize that your personality is just a lens, you begin to shed your default personality patterns. You grip your own lens less tightly and open yourself up to new perspectives and possibility. You begin deepening your understanding of—and relationship with—yourself, which is at the crux of *conscious productivity*: shifting from an externally driven life to an internally driven one.

On the following pages, you'll find a worksheet for you to unpack the Enneagram in more depth and a practice to support you in managing your reactivity. Then it's on to Chapter 3, where we'll talk about goals, ambition, productivity, and *how* you approach your work.

MANAGING REACTIVITY

When you sense yourself getting "hooked" by another person—by something they say or do—or a situation, it's quite common to react unconsciously—meaning, you react and respond on autopilot before you even realize you're doing it. Reactivity is very normal in human interactions *and* it can damage relationships if left unchecked.

Consider how much more potent and fulfilling your connections are when you *do* successfully manage your reactions. Instead of an unconscious reaction, you can respond consciously and authentically, which deepens connection and can strengthen the relationship.

PRACTICE

The next time you feel triggered or hooked by a person or situation, try to follow these steps to manage your reactivity:

1.   Pause.

Practice pausing when you feel and observe yourself becoming emotionally hooked. Taking a pause will shift you immediately from unconscious to conscious. And when you can shift into consciousness, you can intentionally choose your next steps.

Depending on the situation or the trigger, the pause you need may be a few seconds long, a few minutes, or several hours. You may even need to take space away from the situation for a more extended period of time to shift into a clearer, grounded headspace.

When we successfully pause, we're overcoming that initial reaction that comes from the amygdala of our brains, which is the area responsible for the fight-flight-freeze for every person.

2.   Identify.

Take notice of what is going on for you. Name the emotion you're feeling or the sensations you feel in your body. Consider assumptions you may be making. Try to identify what's at the root of your reaction. (Hint: it might be one of the limiting beliefs you identified in Chapter 1.)

This takes practice as well, but the more you practice it, the more skilled you'll become at this step. If you are new to identifying emotions, feelingswheel.com is a great free resource to help you build your emotional vocabulary.

PRACTICE

3. **Determine next steps.**

Once you've paused and identified your assumptions and the root cause, you'll be in a better place to identify what action you need to take next. The more you actively practice observing your reaction, pausing, identifying, and moving forward, the more your brain will recognize your new pattern and your practice will become more natural.

WORKSHEET

THE ENNEAGRAM AND ME

Take a moment to revisit the nine core types of the Enneagram and the areas of over-focus on pages 63 to 65. You can download the workbook at stephaniewoodward.com/resources to access sample worksheets and more Enneagram tools and resources.

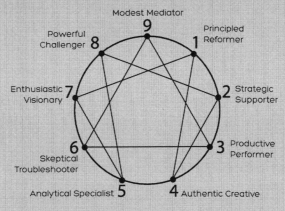

Which of these nine core types do you most identify with?

How do the areas of over-focus for that type relate to the limiting beliefs you identified in Chapter 1?

How does this insight shift your perspective and your limiting beliefs?

WORKSHEET

Bonus

How might your area of over-focus be perceived by the other Enneagram types?

How might you react to the areas of over-focus of the other Enneagram types?

Now that you are conscious of these perceptions, how might it influence your approach with the other Enneagram types?

CHAPTER 3

HOW YOU APPROACH YOUR WORK

What happens when everyone is reinforcing your work life and choices? When everyone is telling you how lucky you are or successful you are? What about when everyone values you because of your role, your status, your work identity? When it becomes hard to separate people liking *you* versus liking your work identity?

And perhaps worst of all, what happens when everyone around you believes you to be a resounding success—you are where they would like to be—and yet you feel unfulfilled, unhappy, perhaps even miserable? When, deep down, where you are spending countless hours every year doesn't feel "right," and you hear internal whispers: *there must be more to (work) life than this.*

AMBITION, HUSTLING, AND CLIMBING THE LADDER

I remember one coworker, early in my career, yelling across the table at me during a team meeting: "You need an attitude of gratitude, young lady!"

I was relatively new to the company and was in a relatively senior role, at a relatively young age. She was none of those things and was exceptionally outraged at my rung on the ladder. I didn't think much of it the first time it happened, but as I progressed in my career, it kept happening, sometimes subtly, sometimes not so subtly. Sometimes in a complimentary way; sometimes in a resentful way.

"How did you get to where you did?"

"Can you come speak on our panel about charting your career path?"

"You took on an executive role so young. Weren't you worried you didn't have the experience to manage those with more experience than you?"

There was this mix of high praise and skepticism, like I was on very shaky ground. One mistake and I could lose it all, so I better follow their advice and do as the system suggested. There was always someone who wanted me to remember that I was young, inexperienced, and needed to be put in my place. The funny thing is, I was very often the person saying that to myself.

I steadily continued the corporate ladder climb, always in my neutral-colored, appropriate-length costume. I continued to deny my own lack of fulfillment, my own dissatisfaction. Interestingly enough, as

I continued to show up in costume and deepen my denial, a series of mysterious food allergies showed up, and within months, I could only tolerate boiled potatoes. I was throwing up everything else.

"Well, there's nothing medically wrong with you," my family physician proclaimed after looking at my blood test results. I just sat there not knowing what to say next. Was I destined to live a life from now on flavored by only boiled potatoes?

Whether she thought it was psychosomatic or an eating disorder, I'll never know. But my osteopath later confirmed that my nervous system was the problem. My parasympathetic nervous system was operating on overdrive, leading to significant inflammation and causing the food sensitivities, essentially an adrenal response that should be reserved for when you're being chased by a bear.

"Let's talk about the stress in your life," she began.

Uh-huh, I thought, *let's*. But instead of making any significant lifestyle changes, I simply budgeted for monthly osteopathic treatments, which would become an expensive bandage for my bleeding nervous system.

* * *

I was a success by everyone's standards. But "success" on whose terms? This was the question that danced around my mind years into my working life. I didn't feel successful. Or fulfilled. Or satisfied.

Those evenings alone with myself in the silence, the same message found me over and over and over again: *What am I doing with my life?* Every night it landed like a thud until eventually I would sit down and beat it to the punch. *I know, I KNOW. I get it.*

But did I? I felt like a brat. An ungrateful, unappreciative brat. How dare I not be happy with this life? *Other people* wanted my job. *Other people* told me how lucky I was. *Other people* were working their asses off to get exactly what I already had.

And then a gentle whisper moved through the back of my mind: *you're not other people. You're you.*

BAH! Why couldn't I just be satisfied with what I had? Why wasn't it good enough? I wanted to put pillows over my ears to stop these whispers, but here was the frustrating part: the whispers were coming from inside me, so there was no escaping them.

Given my level of self-awareness at the time, there was really only one solution at this point. Which was, of course, *ignore and deny these whispers completely.*

After all, what was I going to do? Leave the company? Abandon a role I'd spent years working toward? The whispers were those of a trickster, I decided. A trickster trying to throw me off my game and land me unemployed and unsuccessful. And so I pushed those pesky whispers aside with determination and stubbornness.

My therapist, though, was very curious about these whispers. "What about your life isn't working?" she would ask.

I'd fidget and deflect, frustrated with the question every time. Eventually, though, I'd throw out a series of questions back at her:

I mean, I work really long hours. But doesn't everyone who is ambitious and wants to get ahead?

Sure, I haven't dated anyone meaningful in, well, ever. But I'm still young. And besides, I can't control that, now, can I?

Yeah, I wish I had time for other things sometimes. But I'm a grown adult, and work is work. Life isn't meant to be all fun and games, now, is it?

I noticed her eyebrows rise slightly as she jotted some notes in her notebook. Was I imagining it or was she smiling?

"So, what do you want most right now?" she asked in follow up, meeting my gaze with her steady warmth.

My mind quickly turned to thoughts of work and I responded, "I think I just need to settle into this role, that's all." She stared at me without saying a word, leaving space for me to continue. "I mean, I'm just stressed right now because we've got a lot of new things on the go, and we've got new people on the team . . ."

"So, what you want most right now is to settle into the role?" she repeated in a completely even tone. It was unnerving. What was the right answer? She wasn't letting on. What was it that she wanted to hear? Was I missing something?

"Yes," I said finally, with resolution. "That's what I want."

And so, I set about settling into the role with fierce determination, and just like that, I stuffed those whispers down so far, they were completely inaudible.

Denial is a beautiful thing. I did, in fact, settle into that new role. I continued to see my therapist and my executive coach—our conversations focused on leadership challenges and navigating the corporate ladder. My therapist stopped asking me what I wanted most, and I avoided sitting in the silence (when the whispers would surface) as much as I could.

Instead, I got very busy. I built out my team, quadrupling its size, absorbing other business streams. I set stretch goals and hit them all. One day, I was asked about my career objectives, and if I wanted to put CEO down as my ultimate goal, they would develop and groom me for that position. You'll have to work your ass off, they warned, but that path is possible for you.

Success. Security. Clarity. They were all mine. As I ran my usual forest trail that night, I imagined myself in the CEO role. What would that be like? The word "freedom" jumped immediately to mind and I felt myself puzzle over that reaction. What about the CEO role meant freedom to me? Our CEO worked long hours, took on the toughest board conversations, and navigated the biggest political quandaries. *Freedom?!*

As my feet hit the dirt in their steady rhythmic pattern, the answers started coming . . .

He's the one that sets the pace.

He's the one that sets the budget, the initiatives.

He guides the strategy.

He determines what's good enough.

When he books a vacation, we all revolve around it.

He was the one who set the expectation for the culture, how we worked together, and what was okay and not okay.

I loved this idea of being the chief pacesetter, and the one who determined the working environment.

Huh.

Do I want to be CEO?

I wasn't clear on the answer to that question, but I suddenly started noticing decisions around pacing, budget, strategy, and culture more than ever before. Certain things that had initially felt like annoyances and inconveniences began to really frustrate me. I started noticing when the pace was completely unreasonable, when the pace was determined without a full understanding of the impact on business units. I noticed when my observations about culture were dismissed. I noticed, year after year, the number of initiatives placed on the list, knowing there was no way our company could deliver given our budget and people constraints. I noticed the drop in morale, the turnover, the burnout when we failed to deliver on an impossible number of initiatives year after year. I noticed when I wasn't given full autonomy to manage my team or my calendar. And I really noticed how often my wings were starting to be clipped. Over and over again.

I'm just being groomed, I rationalized to myself.

* * *

Working life continued, and I soon found myself falling into some of my dad's habits: taking time off at (a few) specific occasions, which included Christmas.

The Woodwards did Christmas well. Mostly because we did over-indulging at specific times of the year well. My parents, who were always on some form of diet—be it Scarsdale, Cabbage Soup, Atkins, or Fit for Life—abandoned their restrictions for the nine days between Christmas Eve and New Year's Day. No foods were off limits; no portion too big.

The quantity of overindulgence was always there: twenty-five-plus pound turkey, tin upon tin of Quality Street chocolates; fridge drawers full of cheeses. Bowls of mixed nuts in their shells, which Mum intended mostly as decoration I think, were scattered across the household. We'd rejoice in cracking through those shells, leaving my mum cursing under her breath as she uncovered yet another pile of nutshells in the far corner of some rarely used room in the house.

"Do we have a family of squirrels taking up home in here?" she'd lament, her eyes darting from my sister, to me, to Dad, all of us stifling a giggle. The rule being whoever was holding the nutcracker at Mum's time of entry was to hide it under the sofa cushion behind their back. It was a one-for-all-all-for-one nut snacking pact between the three of us.

The quality of overindulgence improved over the years, matching Dad's growing success and salary. The corner store cheddar once considered a delicacy was replaced by farmer's market Cambozola, Saint Agur, and soft cheeses that would melt to a puddle on the cheese tray if left at room temperature for too long. "All the more reason to eat it quickly!" Dad would explain, winking, as he smeared a glob large enough for three crackers onto a single digestive biscuit and brought it to his mouth. All this for our family of four, which only ever grew to six if a set of grandparents joined us for the holidays from England.

We'd hold ceremony around the pinning of the turkey-taster badge, a plastic orange pin emblazoned with those words and an image of a turkey in a gold lamé finish. The pin rotated every year, each of us getting our turn in four-year cycles. The lucky recipient being the one allowed to take the first official taste of the bird before it was served to everyone else. With every passing year, the gold lamé would lose a degree of luster, the metallic sheen gently being stripped away by loving turkey-greased hands pinning it from one Christmas sweater to another.

At some point, Dad would break into a deep tenor version of "Noel, Noel" or "Good King Wenceslas" as he went to take his seat at the table. We'd pull Christmas crackers, and there Dad would sit, paper crown slightly torn as his monstrous cranium stretched the crown glue beyond its limits, and it always sat askew after his enthusiastic and over-zealous carving of the turkey. It seemed he always pulled a bright crown color: red, yellow, pink. And so it was that my highly revered management consultant dad would be perched at the head of the table, canary-yellow paper crown tipped to his left ear, as he dealt the after-dinner card game in between bites of stilton heaped on a digestive biscuit. This was one of his allowable "off work" times of year, when the track pants came out, his feet kicked up, and he let his office gather dust.

It was my twenty-eighth Christmas and my sister's twenty-second, Mum's fifty-seventh, and Dad's fifty-sixth when it all changed. We sat on edge around the dinner table. The Christmas crackers were pushed aside, wedged between serving plates and the untouched dish of cranberry sauce; mine lay on the floor next to my chair. The turkey-taster badge sat on the kitchen island. No one brought up that it was Dad's year for turkey-tasting first dibs. Mum went back into the kitchen without a word to refill the gravy boat. Sherryl brought forkfuls of turkey, mashed potato, and peas to her mouth, slowly, methodically, her focus on her plate.

I looked over at Dad as he dropped half the turkey on his fork to the table. His eyes were drooped, his face lulled, and it looked as though he might fall forward into his plate.

I'd had it.

Had he become an alcoholic? Like everyone in my family, he'd always enjoyed a few drinks. But it seemed lately he'd either lost his tolerance or had applied the rules of excess to wine and scotch, in addition to the cheese board. His eyes were now often glassy, his temper short, and he couldn't go a day without popping multiple painkillers for a headache he couldn't shake "because of all the work stress." Mum would recite this excuse each time I spoke to her about it. Work stress, my ass, I'd reply to her, if he lay off the pre-dinner scotch maybe he'd suffer fewer headaches.

"Just go to bed, Dad," I said, and slowly raised my eyes from my plate to look across the table at him. There was an edge to my voice that brought everyone to attention at the table. It surprised even me.

Mum shifted uncomfortably in her seat. I avoided making eye contact with my sister, knowing she'd silently implore me to stop talking. The last few months had been excruciating. And I was only there one day a week, as was the family tradition: Sunday night dinner.

He'd been lashing out, screaming at Mum about everything. I looked across the table at him now: What had happened? The man who was once the life of the party could no longer make civil conversation. Drinking made him clumsy and angry. He'd pick fights where once he would have cracked a joke to lighten any intensity at the dinner table. I continued to stare at him, slumped over as he pressed his corn into his mashed potatoes. He'd become unrecognizable, and I realized, as I blinked back tears, I didn't like this man sitting across from me at the table.

None of us said a thing, about his dropped fork or his drooping eyes. We made small talk, finished dinner, and I made an excuse to go back to my apartment that night. I raced to lace up my winter boots, keeping the tears packed away, until I stepped out into the crisp December air and began my walk home.

* * *

As my sister and I walked from the parked car to the hospital entrance, her face was ashen, and I was making every attempt to stay light-hearted and breezy, filling the air with nonsense small talk.

She eventually spoke, her voice uncharacteristically quiet and soft, her gaze cast down at the pavement. "You don't understand, Steph.

You don't live there with him. I do . . ."

I was about to interrupt with statistics, facts, evidence, anything to serve as a plausible reason for his recent demise. Alcohol, stress, mixing alcohol and Advil. But she continued before I could break in. "Something's wrong," she finished, without aggression, without anger, just a frightened sadness lacing her voice. A tone I'd never heard that scared me. My stomach churned, and I had no response.

Dad's headaches had gotten worse, not better, and the sinus medication our family physician had prescribed had done nothing to alleviate the symptoms. Last night, Mum had taken him to the hospital, and she'd called this morning, asking us to come and meet them there as soon as possible. My fear morphed to practicality quickly: get coffee, get muffins, drive car, keep talking. Staying busy and active left no room to replay the call from Mum. I was hoping busyness could erase "something's wrong" from our family's transcript.

With those words erased, I imagined Sher and me walking in to the ER, finding our parents with the emergency room doctors standing next to them, clipboards in hand, sighing, and telling us that they had bigger problems to contend with than a man with a mild drinking problem and stress-induced headaches. *Yes, that's exactly what they'll say*. It brought a smile to my face, and calmness washed over me.

As though reading my mind, Sher interrupted my hospital reverie. "It's not the drinking, Steph. It's not," she said, still not looking at me, as she pulled at a thread on the wrist of her sweater. The thread wasn't loose. She switched tactics, then, and tried pushing the thread back into the sweater, folding the cuff and pushing the left arm of the sweater up her arm to her elbow. "He's not drinking any more or less than he ever has." She let the words just sit there between us.

I stayed silent. There was nothing to say. Accepting her premise would require me to accept a whole new set of possibilities. It was so much easier to blame the drinking.

Finally, I said, "Let's not worry until there's something to worry about." I turned sideways, trying to project a reassuring big-sisterly tone. But her fixed gaze, furrowed brow, and hands dug deep into her pockets told the story I refused to open, read, or listen to.

"It's going to be okay," I said, not recognizing the ridiculousness of such a statement. A promise I will never make to anyone again at any time. "Honestly, it's going to be okay."

There were about twenty paces between the emergency room doors and the patient white board. The board, I learned that morning, was where each patient who was admitted to the emergency room and was waiting for a hospital bed was listed. The patient names were on the left and their corresponding ailment was scribbled in the right-hand column. At first, it was hard to decipher the names; they were written in various dry-erase-board-marker colors—green, red, blue, black. There were also remnants of chicken scratch handwriting, where nurses in a rush had used their hand or elbow to wipe off one name to replace it with another, leaving the arc of a "c" or tail of a "t" behind in the chaos.

"Steph—" Sher's voice rang out, and her finger pointed up at the board, landing next to Dad's name, written in blue. His was the fifth name down from the top. They had lost interest with the "r" at the end of "Christopher" so it read more as the French "Christophe." The marker had clearly started to run out halfway through "Woodward," so the "ard" was finished in green.

Next to his name, scribbled in the adjacent column, were the letters "BT." Those two letters, B and T, written no bigger and no smaller than "appendix" and "hernia" marked in the rows above and below his.

BT. I felt a thud in my stomach, as though I'd been punched and the fist grabbed hold of my insides and started tugging. Tugging at my lungs, my throat, at everything. I could feel the blood rush from my face to my stomach, and I put my hand on the wall as I felt the room start to spin.

My sister's voice came as though through a haze. "Brain tumor. Fuck. Steph, it's a brain tumor." Her hand closed over her mouth and she bent forward slightly.

Her voice brought me back into focus. "We don't know that," I heard myself say. Right, it could mean anything. *Blood transfusion. Yes! Blood transfusion. That must be it.*

"Where are they?" I muttered partly to my sister, partly to myself, partly to the nurses buzzing through the halls. "Where are they?" I repeated loudly this time, my voice edged to hysteria, my eyes scanned the hall in panic, and I began scouring the temporary patient rooms that made up the emergency room corridor.

I started walking down a hallway, taking in patient names as I went. "Woodward. Christopher Woodward," I said, tugging at a nurse's sleeve. "Where is he?" The nurse looked both shocked and annoyed and pulled herself free from my tug. She muttered something about room numbers being listed on the board, but I was already moving past her, scanning names outside of the curtain walls that made up the makeshift rooms of the emergency room.

As we approached the curtain that read "Woodward" outside, I heard the treble of my mum's voice. I pulled back the curtain and there they were—Mum and Dad—waiting. Dad in his dressing gown from home. Their coats and sweaters were draped over a plastic chair in the corner, their faces white, their smiles forced. Dad's eyes told a very different story. My dad, who'd always joked about his fearless-ness—that he wasn't afraid of anything, anything!—was scared. Really scared. The bag of muffins fell from my hand to the plastic chair at the foot of the bed.

And I knew then: it wasn't the drinking. And it wasn't going to be okay.

My dad had a stage 4 incurable brain tumor. Life expectancy: two months to two years.

* * *

I called work from the hospital, reporting my dad's prognosis as specifically as the doctors had explained it to me. My voice was robotic: the terms I uttered, technical. I gave no space for anyone to ask questions, clarify, or empathize. I wanted to get through this report as quickly as possible and never speak of it again.

It was then I realized that while it seemed like it had been weeks, months, several lives, since Dad's diagnosis, for the rest of the world, only thirty-eight hours had passed. I hadn't yet missed a day of work.

My apologetic tone and promises of catching up on missed emails and reporting were premature.

On the other end of the line, my boss stammered and fumbled, not quite knowing what to say. Could I blame him? I'd called on a Sunday night unannounced and versed him on glioblastoma brain tumors.

"Will you be in tomorrow?" he finally asked, likely a default response. I was speechless. I wanted to say yes. I wanted everything to be as it was. To wake up tomorrow, make coffee, jump on the subway at 7:15 in the morning, and banter with Mike as I worked my way through the morning office shenanigans. And then I wanted to laugh about some ridiculous thing Mary would find on the internet and stress over whether I could get all the way to the Japanese takeout at lunch and make it back to my meeting in time. I wanted to put the finishing touches on the board report before it got sent out.

I wanted life to go on as normal.

"I don't think so," I said, my voice a murmur. "I, uh, think my family needs me . . ." the words sounded foreign and strange. I'd never used a phrase like that before. My family had never been one to *need* me, certainly not when there was work to get done or a deadline looming.

"Of course, of course," he replied quickly, and I could picture him shaking his head, trying to scramble and un-utter the words he had just spoken. I was about to hang up when I heard him on the other end, "Oh, Stephanie!" his voice rang out.

"Yeah?"

"The annual report. Where are we on that? Is it in good shape? You know, just in case I get asked."

The question jolted me. I closed my eyes and tried to shake the grogginess out of them as I mentally flicked through the work files of my mind.

The annual report . . . The annual report . . .

My brain shifted in to regular gear and I spoke about the president's letter and the strategy outline. They both needed work. That the print files were on my desk. In a purple folder. He sounded confused and overwhelmed and so I slowed my tone and repeated that the folder was purple. And on my desk. And if he couldn't find it or had questions to call me.

"Thanks. Okay, yeah. Got it," he said. "You're the best." The phone clicked and he was gone.

* * *

"You're looking too skinny" one of the women at the office commented as I walked in one morning. I cast her a sideways glance, dismissive, and kept walking for my office. I sat down at my desk with a slight wince, my thighs still burning from my run the night before. I'd started running greater distances. It was the only thing these days that could clear my head, to keep me from screaming or crying. When I didn't think about Dad's failing body or the deadlines I was missing at work.

It was thirty days since Dad's diagnosis.

The computer hummed itself to life and the update notices, anti-virus security badges, flashed across the screen as it booted up.

There was a soft rap at my office door and I looked up to see Karen standing there. My boss's EA. She was tentative as she spoke up, her words soft and apologetic, "I was, umm, just wondering . . . no rush, of course . . . if . . . the committee report is . . . maybe done? Or going to be done today . . .?" her voice trailed off as she caught my blank stare. "Or even just an idea of when it might be done?"

In some way, I wished no one at the office knew that Dad was so ill. The tentative words and the pained, sometimes terrified, expressions of sympathy were plenty. Or those who had lost loved ones to cancer who would show up at my office door, their eyes flooded with tears, who thought I wanted to swap stories of heartbreak. Then there were those who tiptoed around me, with a tentative cadence, hoping to not have to interact with me at all. It all just served as a reminder.

And yet the demands and aggression of those who didn't know felt overwhelming and sent me into a tailspin. This desperate sadness, it turned out, was illogical. I didn't know how to work this way. I didn't recognize myself.

"Today," I said to Karen, with more confidence than I felt. "I'll get it done today."

I sat in that office, tucked away in the corner, for hours, just tapping away. The repetitive clicks, soothing, meditative. Ignoring the hushed whispers outside my door, the reminders of the other deadlines, I clacked away at that committee report—until the sun dipped below the horizon.

* * *

When I joined the workforce, no one talked about mental health out-side of the obligatory mental health training workshops that taught managers how to navigate conversations about short- and long-term leaves of absence and return-to-work accommodation policies. That was it. The idea that fluctuations in mental health are natural for *all* employees wasn't on anyone's radar. Including my own. In fact, my radar would have repelled the idea. I was of the "suck it up, buttercup" mentality. Especially for myself. Back at this point in my life when I was still living very unconsciously and separate from my own inner truth, I didn't have time for feelings, and I certainly didn't believe in taking time off work for anything other than a debilitating flu or surgery.

And so, as I repressed and pushed down the emotions that were doing everything they could to pop up—to help me process, integrate, and accept that my dad was dying—my brain was becoming foggier and foggier, my sleep non-existent. I would toss and turn all night, and push my way through the workday, pretending like I was the same Stephanie I had been only a month earlier.

I wasn't, of course. I would be again, but at that time, in that moment of intense grief, I was not myself. My headspace was unrecognizable to me. I struggled to connect the dots between thoughts. I processed things more slowly. I was easily distracted, easily irritated. My pace of work slowed. But take time off? Absolutely not. *Good employees don't take time off*, went the ingrained-belief refrain train through my mind.

Besides, what would I do? Sit at home and cry? Stare at Dad in bed as he slowly lost functionality? This idea seemed preposterous at the time. Now, sitting here writing these words, my today self holds back tears and thinks: *yes, that's exactly what would have served you best.* It would have been devastatingly painful—sometimes it is much more comfortable to live in distraction and denial—but it would have honored an incredibly difficult time and allowed me to process the truth of what was happening, instead of repressing it and choosing to power ahead and living with the consequence of that decision.

* * *

Another week passed. Dad couldn't walk. He'd lost all muscle tone in his legs from the steroids that were keeping the fluid off his brain and reducing the swelling caused by the tumor. I decided to temporarily move into the spare bedroom in my parents' home. It seemed like the right thing to do, despite the fact that I was the world's worst caregiver. I'd forget how many pills he'd been given and when. I was a terrible cook, and my mum didn't want us living off takeout food.

And so my contribution was staying calm and taking on the emotional needs of the family. I also took my dad's business calls, letting clients know that he was ill and in the hospital and would be in touch as soon as possible. I took notes at every doctor's visit, documenting every comment, every update, every new aspect of the illness. I was an expressionless, ever-available sounding board for anyone wanting to cry or vent, pushing my own tears, fears, and anger to the background.

At work, the annual report deadline was fast approaching and so being in the office was necessary. I'd leave my parents' house, commute to work, and check in with my mum every hour. This particular day, I had a status update meeting with my boss.

As I walked into his office, his face visibly changed. He looked shocked. Or was it pity? "How are things?" he asked uncomfortably as he shifted in his chair. I looked tired, that was a given. I'd barely been sleeping. After documenting the doctor's description of the radiation process, I'd had nightmares of lasers burning through my brain. When that became intolerable—waking me up every hour—the nightmares shifted to insomnia.

"I'm fine," I said with a nod, ignoring the voice that begged me to go back home and sleep. "All good." I pretended to be looking for a specific paper in the pile of papers I had in my lap. "You know, Mum is having a tough time . . . I'm worried about her." My boss said nothing in response, and so I kept talking. "The doctors have confirmed it's terminal. The radiation and chemo will only extend his life, at best . . ." and I continued, without pause, for twenty minutes. Spewing every detail. My boss just stared back at me until my diatribe came to an end.

"I'm, uh, really sorry," he stuttered. I wished I hadn't said anything; he looked pained trying to respond. I looked down at the papers and pushed my shoe across the floor, tracing an invisible infinity pattern. "Look," he finally continued, "HR has told me to offer you time off . . ." his voice trailed off and my eyes snapped from the floor, and my shoe, back up to his.

"But I—" I started to interject, but he cut me off almost immediately.

"To be honest, she didn't ask me to *offer* it to you. . . ." It was his turn to now shuffle papers across his desk, his eyes avoided mine. "They, um, asked me to *tell* you to, uh . . ." his voice dropped and it felt like minutes passed before he finished the sentence. "To *tell* you to take time off."

The words landed like a thud. I felt a mild panic. I thought about sitting at home watching Dad struggle to move and watching Mum struggle even more to move him. I imagined watching family friends stop by, seeing their faces change as they took in Dad's condition for the first time: their winces, their fear, their shock. The panic gripped my stomach, and I thought I might throw up right there on the annual report mock-up. I couldn't do it. I didn't want to sit at home.

"But I don't want time off!" I protested "I, well, I, um, I can't just . . ." I didn't know how to finish the sentence. I can't just sit at home trying not to cry all day. I can't let myself—my life—just fall apart. No. I needed structure. I needed files. And reports. And order. "No." I said, finally, "I don't want time off."

The relief swept across his eyes. This was clearly the response he wanted to hear. "Okay, good. Good." He looked up, met my gaze, and smiled. "Very good. I mean, of course, when you need to be with your family, we'll accommodate for that—" he started speaking more quickly, excitedly, "and we can adjust the projects you're on." He began making notes in his notebook. "But yes, I agree it makes sense for you to be here." He paused and his face grew resolute. "It will be a good distraction, I'm sure."

In that moment, it felt like my boss understood me better than anyone else in the world. The last thing I needed was to sit with my feelings, locked in the house, watching my dad deteriorate. That would be lunacy. I needed distraction. I needed a place where my emotions couldn't find me, chase me down, and force me to pay attention. Our status update continued on, business as usual, and I felt relieved to be documenting my marching orders, rather than prescription details.

* * *

Dad's life expectancy reduced with every doctor's visit. The projected timelines kept changing, the doctors sounding no different from the project managers at work updating the executive team on changes to the schedule for an IT project. I'd been the one keeping notes at every doctor's visit and documenting every emergency, every prescription, every side effect, and every treatment option.

We were back in the hospital. A storm escalated outside, the claps of thunder eclipsing the beep of the heart monitor each time they rumbled. In those precious few seconds, I could almost see the dad who napped on the couch in the basement—a power nap before guests arrived for the annual company barbeque; an exhausted pass out after a long week at work; a boozy-induced midafternoon snooze by the pool. And then the thunder passed and the beeping resumed. And there we were, keeping vigil bedside following another emergency surgery.

Dad's face had become misshapen—bloated, puffy, and pale—in a way that was textbook, the doctors had explained, for a brain tumor at this stage, being treated in this way. I had become accustomed to it. And when he was awake, my focus was always his eyes. And the rise and fall of his chest as he slept.

His breathing was sporadic and disturbed. Especially that night. Mum hadn't slept in over forty-eight hours. I told her she had to go home, that I would take the overnight shift. I hadn't stayed overnight yet at the hospital, but I knew it was necessary. Mum needed to sleep. And Dad . . . someone needed to be here. For once, Mum didn't argue with me.

Tonight could be the night he dies.

I hid my terror at being alone in the room with him and the monitor by giving Mum a hug and immediately turned away and busied myself by clearing the paper coffee cups by the sink and straightening the already flat sheet by Dad's left foot. Meanwhile, she rhymed off instructions in one flurried run-on sentence, "Don't leave the room the doctors will do rounds and they do them at all hours of the night if you leave for a second you could miss them and we won't know how he's doing and ask about his sugar levels remind them of the diabetes sometimes they won't see that on the chart . . ."

My mind absorbed each individual word while at the same time floating above the words, in a misty surreal kind of way, connecting no real meaning to them as they strung together. The exhaustion and the fear began pooling over my left brow and pushed a searing pain through my head. I needed her to leave before I fully fell apart. Alone in this room, I could hold space for my own feelings and fear. I didn't have the capacity to hold hers as well.

She left, and I folded over in the plastic chair. I tried to steady my thoughts by cupping my head in my hands and pinching my cheeks. The hospital room floor was speckled but not enough to hide the dust bunnies that ran along the baseboards and bumped up against the myriad of electrical cords connecting the monitors to power. A nurse pushed an empty bed out in the hallway, creating enough of a breeze to nudge the dust over the cords, and I followed the light gray ball as it shimmied its way gracefully across the floor. It finally settled against the leg of the makeshift desk we'd created in the far corner of the room. I walked over, put my shoe over the ball and pressed it into the floor. I did the same to the dust bunny next to it, and then the one next to it, until I'd circled the room, crushing every bunny that dared to dance by those monitor cords.

I looked over at Dad. The monitor beeped, his chest rose, the thunder clapped. This steady chorus continued as I wedged a tissue under my shoe and pulled it around the edges of the room, sweeping up the dust bunny remains. My foot came to a stop as it bumped back up against the desk, having gone full circle around the room. I tossed the now-gray tissue into the garbage. The monitor beep marked the seconds as I settled in next to the desk and picked up the folder Mum had prepared, which held every instruction, prescription, symptom, and surgery, with dates and outcomes highlighted in yellow in the margins. Next to the folder was a Tim Hortons cup filled with pens. I pulled a thin black one from the cup and turned to the page with the hourly log and began jotting notes. My elbow slipped as I wrote, causing me to scribble a long line across the page. The small side table that we'd declared a desk had not made it so—it was intended to hold cups of ice chips, not office supplies and the weight of arms writing cursive notes into medical files. As I closed the folder, the corner knocked the Tim Hortons cup and the pens fell to the floor.

Thunder. Beep. Silence. Beep. Silence. Beep. Silence. Thunder.

I looked at Dad, unmoving, unrecognizable. The desperation I felt fired upward and stung the back of my eyes until the pressure pushed through and a sob rippled through my body and tore through my throat as the tears dropped.

Please just give me one more minute to talk to him. Please. One more minute. I need to tell him I'm sorry. I need to tell him I love him.

All I could think about was business school. How disappointed he had been. How he hadn't spoken to me properly for over a year. I needed to know why, and I needed to know that he had forgiven me. That he was proud of me now.

Thunder crackled again and the room brightened as the flash of lightening illuminated the metal and white surroundings. I reached over the hospital bed armrest with both hands and let my forehead fall into the cradle of my arms and slipped into sleep.

When I awoke, the sun was piercing through the slats in the hospital blinds, casting stripes across the room. The rays danced around the room and formed a pinstripe pattern across Dad's forearm. There was no trace of the thunder or storm of the night before. The monitor continued its staccato, Dad's chest rose and fell, and I looked at him then, the man who'd barely spoken to me for a year after that fateful business school decision.

I rested my hand over his and squeezed it gently. "I just wanted you to understand me, Dad, to care about what I wanted," I whispered. "That's all I wanted."

And in the silent space between the beeps, it was as though his mind placed the response into my head: *I only knew how to want for you,* it seemed to say, *what I wanted for myself.*

LIMITING BELIEFS AND PERSONALITY PATTERNS

To this day, it pains me to think of that moment next to Dad in the hospital. As he lay there, terminally ill, all I could think about was whether he'd forgiven me for giving up my spot at business school. *That* was what consumed my thoughts during that time: whether that external goal—that I had long since moved passed—remained a sticking point between me and my dying father.

That is the power of limiting beliefs and the external validation drive of *unconscious productivity*. My worth, at the time, was completely wrapped up in what I produced and how high I climbed. Not only that, but I then needed my Dad to confirm that what I was now producing and the height to which I'd climbed was worthy of his approval.

Did he consider my current success good enough to override my decision to study psychology instead of pursuing an HBA? I was desperate for this confirmation. And in the absence of that confirmation—given that he wasn't capable of processing that type of question at that stage of his illness—what did I do? I worked harder. And longer. Instead of spending quality time with him in those final months—sharing memories, having some laughs, or listening to music together—I worked harder and longer in one final effort to make him proud.

I also remember my body crying out to me during that time. It wanted a chance to process the diagnosis. To let emotions run their course. Instead, I pushed them down, ignoring them completely.

Remember the key challenge for Enneagram Type 9s? It's

self-forgetting. Forgetting my own perspective, my own needs, and remaining focused on everything, anything, and anyone else.

It was these limiting beliefs and personality patterns that kept me cycling in the painful loop of unconscious productivity during one of the toughest times in my life, keeping me hooked into work and external goals rather than focusing on my family life and processing what I was about to lose.

GOALS, AMBITION, AND PRODUCTIVITY

Goals, ambition, and productivity—your relationship with these three things will certainly influence your work experience, and your life as a whole. Up until this point in my life, goals, ambition, and productivity shaped every decision in my life. And since I placed all of my focus on work, my goals were all career-oriented. As soon as I achieved one professional goal, I was setting a new one. As soon as I reached a particular standard of excellence and competence, I pushed the bar higher. Once one role was earned, there was another one to strive for.

Perhaps you've held a specific career-related goal for yourself from a young age. Perhaps your parents or other influential individuals in your life held a specific career goal for you and guided you along that path. Your Enneagram type and limiting beliefs may also provide some insight on what you prioritize professionally, and how you define your relationship with ambition and productivity.

All of this shapes what you expect from your career, your organization, and yourself, as well as how you show up in the workplace, how you relate to your colleagues, how you lead, and how you follow.

Clients coming into my coaching practice show up with a myriad of topics—but they center around their experience of work. Some come in questioning whether they are in the right role and industry. Some are having interpersonal issues with a boss, colleagues, or direct reports. Others come in questioning how all the different pieces of their life fit together: Have they over-prioritized work? Are they over-prioritizing their personal life? Sometimes, they feel they are failing at both and are craving a deeper understanding of what it means to feel balanced in their lives.

The common thread between many of my clients is that there's some sense of unfulfillment, untapped potential, and a strong desire for change. They're willing and open to making those changes, but they don't know where to start.

THE HUSTLE

We've all heard of hustle culture. It speaks to a lifestyle defined by overworking; to feel compelled to always be working harder, faster, and stronger; when work becomes such a priority in your life or in the environment in which you work that the other aspects of your life are pushed aside. Feelings of "grind" and "burnout" are associated with hustle culture.

Hustle culture is intricately connected with unconscious productivity—when we're setting goals (or being handed goals) and are gauging our self-worth by how much we produce against those goals in a day, *as determined by external others.* You may find yourself constantly comparing your goals, your accomplishments to others.

Too much unconscious productivity—hustle, unconscious ambition, busy for busy's sake—can drive us to burnout. **Without conscious reflection, you can end up on a very busy, achieving, and productive path that leads you directly to unfulfillment**.

You may be feeling some strong reactions at this point. When I start talking about over-work, over-prioritizing work, burnout, and grind, I'm met with a range of emotions from full-out resistance and outrage: "But I love my job! It's an important part of my identity!" to penny-dropping realization, usually accompanied by sadness: "I'm working so hard and I'm so tired and I'm missing out on my life."

I work with a significant number of mid- to senior- level executives in my coaching practice, all of whom are "successful" by conventional definitions. They're earning good salaries and hold impressive roles and titles. *And yet they never feel like they are doing or accomplishing enough.* It's fairly common for workplaces to encourage ten-plus hour days, evening work, and weekend work. Dedication and commitment to the organization is directly tied to their level of hustle and how busy and productive they remain. And how many hours they log.

Some organizations that are more progressive recognize that hours logged do not necessarily result in better outcomes and yet . . . unless you are exhibiting real signs of burnout or making errors, rarely would you hear a boss or colleague say, "Hey, maybe you're working too much."

Long hours still tend to be worn like a badge of honor, and we still tend to regale the employees who log evening and weekend hours, even though working at this ongoing pace is out of sync with our human biology and isn't a sustainable way to achieve results and outcomes. As humans, we are not designed as machines to work at full capacity, every day, for decades.

Even though we know our bodies are not designed for this pace of work, I still hear the guilt—and hints of failure—in people's voices when they confess to being tired or craving rest and restoration. They'll feel lazy or think there is something wrong with them when they can't sustain their energy, productivity, and a frenetic pace over the longer term. Let alone desire all the things they are missing out on in their non-work life.

You can get caught in a dangerous loop, thinking: *If I don't maintain this pace, I'm a failure. And yet, this pacing is leading to dissatisfaction in my life.*

My over-identification with work, hustle mentality, and "suck it up, buttercup" approach to my own physical and mental health made me very successful at work.

Of course, it would. I placed no limits on my work capacity. I had no boundaries—personal or professional. Organizations love this. They won't tell you they love this, however. If asked explicitly, they'll say, outraged, "Of course we want our people to be healthy!"

There are few companies (though shockingly there are some) that will openly admit to not caring about their employees' well-being, but here's the thing: No one will stop you from workaholism or burnout.

No one. (Except perhaps your therapist.)

You over-identifying with your work and sacrificing things that are critical to you, like your health or your family won't be noticed by anyone . . . but you.

YOUR OWN DEFINITION OF AMBITION AND SUCCESS

Ambition can be a double-edged sword. Considered through the lens of *conscious productivity*, it can help us articulate and manifest what we truly wish to do, create, and experience in our lives. Considered through the lens of *unconscious productivity*—the world of comparison, external validation, and striving—it can propel you into a life of not-enough-ness and unfulfillment.

What comes to mind for you when you think of ambition?

- Big, lofty career goals?
- A friend who wanted to be a CEO by the age of 35?
- Starting your own business?
- Having a certain amount of money in the bank by a certain time?
- A desire to climb the corporate ladder as high as possible?

In my experience, ambition is typically linked with the unconscious productivity loop: external comparison and perpetual striving. Those I've met who self-identify as ambitious tend to be forever striving. Rarely do they feel satisfied with where they are. Once they've achieved one goal, they are on to the next.

So, here's a question: *Is there anything wrong with that?*

Perhaps you've already guessed from the personal stories I've shared to this point that my 20-something self would be yelling out: *Of course not!*

But over time, I've come to a different conclusion. The definition of "ambitious" is "*having or showing a strong desire and determination to succeed.*" Nowhere in that definition does it speak to a particular title, wrung on the ladder, or salary level. I'd argue that we've just been conditioned to associate "success" with those things.

So, really, ambition comes down to your definition of success.

When I talk about unconscious productivity, I'm talking about when goal setting and ambition are on autopilot, based on conditioning. When you accept *others'* definition of success as your own. The shift to conscious productivity is to commit to deciding what success means to *you*. Success on your own terms.

Perhaps if my definition of success back in the day had included "quality time with family" or "managing my health," I may not have worked instead of being with my dad in his final months. I may not have continually ignored my body's warning signs and given myself proper rest instead.

When in the unconscious productivity loop, my definition of success was costing me a well-rounded, healthy, joyful life.

What is your definition of success costing *you?* That's where we're headed in the next chapter.

REFLECTION

HOW YOU APPROACH YOUR WORK

Spend a moment to reflect on how you approach your work. Here are some questions for you to consider:

- Who are your external validators (or whose approval do you most seek)?

- Who do you most often compare yourself to?

- How do you define ambition and success for yourself?

- In what ways are you hooked to unconscious productivity?

CHAPTER 4

WHAT IS IT COSTING YOU?

Even when my dad was dying of cancer, with a terminal diagnosis, I resorted to my default work habits and resisted any attempts to slow my pace and engage meaningfully with my life outside of work. At the time, this *truly* felt like the most comfortable and reasonable choice.

* * *

Back at the office, I sat with my office door barely ajar. The words on the computer screen were fuzzy. I was exhausted.

Is it Monday or Tuesday today?

I pulled out the moss-green hospital journal and opened it to the latest entry from the doctor's visit two days ago, dated May 15: "RADI-ATION NOT TAKING. 2 WEEKS." was written in capital letters and hidden slightly behind a receipt for a Tim Hortons coffee that was wedged into the crease of the notebook page.

Two weeks.

The words reverberated through my mind, but wouldn't stick and compute. I stared at my computer screen through what felt like layers of mist and fog. With the latest timeline, I struggled to focus, to find my composure. My body shook as I recalled this latest meeting with the oncologist, holding the pen over the notebook, my hand trembling and unable to drop to the page. There were no medications to document, no follow up appointments to record, no medical trials to consider; just a phone number and doctor recommendation for the switch to palliative care.

Following that meeting, as though operating from a trance, I called my boss and let him know that I would come to the office the next day, gather my files, send emails, make phone calls, and close off my work. It was as though I was headed on a long vacation.

Except I'm leaving to watch my dad die.

I shook my head, hoping the motion would shake up the tension and alleviate my headache. It didn't. My boss, of course, had said all the right things: condolences, offers of help, sympathy to my family at this difficult time, and utterances of "take all the time you need."

I turned back to my computer. Coming in to the office "the next day" had turned into the next day and the day after. It was now May 17th, and I rushed to close everything: to clear the files from my desk, sign all the paperwork, get everything in order. It seemed endless. And . . . there was a part of me that wanted it to be endless. To never leave this desk, this office. Never go home, where Dad lay in a rented medical bed in the living room, on the main floor of the house. He'd begun babbling incoherently, going in and out of consciousness, and last night he hadn't wanted to eat.

I'm scared to go home.

I was scared to be at his bedside counting down the days. Flipping through the paperwork at my desk, there was structure. I could hold the pen and feel the familiar glide of my signature across the page.

The desktop phone started ringing, and I saw my parents' landline number flash across the screen.

Mum.

She had been in a flurry the last two days, arranging all the palliative care we would need at home for the next few weeks. I didn't want to pick up the phone, didn't want to hear about the latest emergency, the medical details, the symptoms. I couldn't, wouldn't, document the death of my dad.

"Hi, Mum," I said softly into the receiver. "I'm just closing things down. I'll be home for dinner," I added quickly, assuming that was the confirmation she wanted.

Instead, her breath was quite labored. "Stephie, you need to come home," she said, slight panic edging her voice.

"Yes, I know. I'm just finishing things up, and then I'm leaving for good—"

Mum cut me off. "The doctor is here. Your dad . . . he's stopped drinking. He can't swallow. They . . . he—" her voice caught. Was she crying? In the months of the illness, I hadn't seen her cry.

"Mum?" my voice trembled slightly and fear darted around my mind.

What is happening?

"He only has hours," she said firmly, and swallowed any tears that might have been coming. "Come home now."

"Hours? Mum . . . what?"

"Now! Come Home Now!" she yelled into the phone.

"I'm coming. I'm coming," I stammered and hung up the phone. I stood up, sat back down again, and stood up. I started walking to the door to grab my bag off the back hook and instead crashed into the side of my desk, sending a sharp pain through my hip. My knees and hands were shaking and I couldn't grasp my bag. I steadied myself by putting a hand on my desk. I felt myself push the shaking, the tears, the fear to a compartment in my mind. I switched to autopilot, cruise control. I began methodically gathering my belongings—laptop, cell phone, crumb-filled Ziploc bag leftover from lunch, and switched from my office heels to my flip-flops.

Calling a taxi didn't occur to me. *Why didn't I call a taxi?* Instead, I got on the subway, as if I were commuting home like any other day of the week. Looking around the subway car, I listened as though through a thick fog to people as they complained about the weather, about their boss, about feeling tired, about their impending exam, about their mother-in-law. Someone was even laughing. The poster on the wall across from me announced a new clinic that promised discretion for all your cosmetic surgery needs.

Approaching my stop, I lost focus and walked right into a man leaning against the wall by the subway doors. "Watch it!" he hissed, narrowing his eyes to slits as he shot me a look of disgust. I half-stumbled from the train onto the platform.

As I stepped out from underground, I heard my Blackberry buzz. It was a note from my boss, forwarding me the announcement that the annual report was now live. "I know you've left, but what's the next step?" was the note he'd attached to the forward. I was a three-minute walk still from my parents' home, the May sun streaming down on me from above. Resting my bag on the sidewalk next to me, I hit reply on the email and jotted down the action items he needed to do. "I'll touch base again in an hour," I wrote, pressed send, and finished the walk.

As I approached the front door, I felt like I was floating above myself and the entire scene, the scene of a girl about to walk in to a makeshift hospital.

He can't swallow. He has hours left. Come Home Now.

I turned the doorknob, and as the door swung open, I heard the voices of my mum, aunt, and cousin ring out and fill the space around me. "Stephie's home," Mum called out to Dad. "She's home!" My mum's face looked strained as she rushed to the door, waved me inside, reached to pull my sleeve. She turned back to the doctor then and ignored my sleeve. She went motionless.

"He's gone," the doctor announced. They wrote down the time of death: 5:47 p.m.

"He was waiting for you to come home," my aunt said, reading the thoughts in my own mind. And the scene before my eyes went black as I dropped to the living room floor, wedged between the medical bed and the ottoman, and the sobs coursed out of and through me like waves. I felt my aunt and my cousin rubbing my back, and still the tears poured forth. The world was black. My dad was gone.

* * *

My executive coach sat across from me at our regular table at the coffee shop where we met on a monthly basis. It was a table tucked into the far corner, wedged between the window and the doorway. I didn't need her concerned expression to remind me of how awful I looked. I was well aware. I felt tired and shaken to my very bones. Meeting her gaze, I felt untethered and unsettled.

"Stephanie," she began gently. "I want you to take time for yourself." I stared back at her blankly.

"Your dad has just died. You're under massive deadline at work. I'm concerned it's too much." She paused before continuing. "I *know* it's too much. I'm recommending—"

"No!" I said, several decibels too loudly, as people at the nearby tables turned to stare. I gritted my teeth and softened my voice. "What am I going to do? Huh? Sit at home and cry?" I let the question hang in the air between us, waiting for her to respond. She didn't. "I'm not going to sit at home and cry. It won't bring him back. And it won't help."

I then shifted the conversation and began ranting about a project and a colleague who just didn't fully grasp the scope of the latest initiative.

She patiently nodded her head, the crease in her forehead steadily deepening. And was it just me or were her eyes welling up?

I kept talking.

"Steph," she interjected at the end, again in that patient, soft voice of hers, and she put her hand on mine. "I'm going to introduce you to my colleague. She's a therapist. The company is going to pay for it."

And just like that, I began seeing a therapist.

* * *

I visited Sonia, my new therapist, every two to four weeks. I was now in *therapy,* a concept both foreign and somewhat unwelcome, and not at all aligned with my British upbringing.

One of my very first assignments was to sit in the quiet.

I had never experienced real heartbreak—real devastation—until this point, I confided in one of my sessions. Furthermore, I'd also been fortunate to never have a significant hit to my mental health until this point. But, I'd continued, my "suck it up, buttercup" mentality no longer working. Suddenly my mind was a fog; I couldn't follow along in meetings like I used to. I had chronic insomnia. My dad's death consumed my thoughts.

She asked about work and how they were supporting me, and I immediately came to my boss's defense. My executive was doing a great job, I said firmly. But looking back, I think it was mostly because we shared the same *beliefs.* And at the time, my belief was: it's best to distract and consume myself with work rather than sit at home crying on the couch. Work was at the core of my identity. I had no idea who I was outside of work, so it was my comfort zone. Mental and emotional health be damned; I was going to go back to my comfort zone. And let's be honest, that suited my executive and my organization just fine.

And they were wonderful and patient, *but* I still showed up. I still got my core responsibilities done.

My therapist listened to this with patience and empathy, then assigned me my homework: I was to sit in the quiet—with no distractions—for an hour every night after work. No TV, no phone calls, no book. Just sit with my own company for an hour. Every day.

Pfft, I thought, *how hard could that be?*

In the silence, I thought about leaving the house. I thought about fetching a glass of wine, but her instructions had been clear: no alcohol during the quiet time.

So, there I sat, in the silence, with a glass of water.

My stomach rumbled, and I thought about the empty fridge.

I wanted to open my computer and jot down some notes for the meeting tomorrow.

I thought about calling a colleague to commiserate about the upcoming work deadlines.

On the other side of the wall, I heard my neighbor calling to his kids downstairs, and then the whirr of an electric toothbrush. One of his boys brushing their teeth before bed. I'd heard this bedtime routine almost every night since I'd bought the place. Across the wall, I could hear him yell out, "Pick a book each . . . ONE each," and then came the noise of their running footsteps, clapping the hardwood floors above as they ran to their bookcase.

I stared at my computer, perched on the far end of the coffee table. I would go into work tomorrow like I had for so many years. To the same people, the same files, the same clients, the same demands, the same deadlines. And yet, I was different. I doodled on the notepad I had within arm's reach, writing a "28" and a "57": my age and Dad's age. Twenty-eight was Dad's middle age.

What if this is my middle age? What am I doing?

I looked around at my empty, perfectly styled home. There was no mess because there was no one here to mess it up. No one to make dinners for, or eat dinners with, and therefore no dishes to clean. My fridge was filled with takeout. My floor littered with work files. I couldn't remember the last time I'd taken a vacation or gone on a meaningful date.

I took another long sip of water and let my head fall back against the couch cushion.

What am I doing with my life?

That night, I was fidgety within eight minutes.

Just sit here. Just stop. Pause. Breathe.

And so I took a deep breath. Or at least, I tried. The breath didn't want to come all the way in. It felt stuck. Shallow. Too much effort to bring it all the way down, like it was getting caught at my heart. I tried again. Same thing.

My heart was catching its breath.

Almost immediately, I felt a sadness trickle up and over me as I looked around the house. I'd bought this house a year ago—with my own savings, with no help from anyone—and it represented all the hard work, all the hours, all the sacrifices I'd made. But now, when I looked around—everywhere I looked—all I could see were pristine surfaces. My kitchen counters: immaculate. *I never cook.* My fridge:

empty, except for a wedge of cheese and half an avocado. My weights and fitness gear: unused in the corner. *When was the last time I did a really good workout?*

But what really struck me: I was all alone. There was no one else here to make a mess. Or create any chaos. Or put their leftovers in the fridge. Or cook leftovers to go in the fridge! No one's plates to litter the countertops. No closet space to divvy up.

Sure, I'd dated. I'd had relationships. But nothing meaningful or memorable. There was no good-one-who-got-away in my past. The truth was: I'd never put the time in to find a good one or created the space for a good one to come into my life.

I'd been working nonstop since the day I graduated.

I had become a loyal workhorse. Place the directive in front of me, and I delivered. I wouldn't let the team down. Good ole reliable, high-performing Steph.

She'll finish the brief.

She'll get us across the finish line.

She doesn't mind finishing it up tonight.

And I'd lapped it all up. Like the kid slurping a Coke in the basement bar with Dad. I'd loved the praise. I loved being the one that everyone counted on.

I was becoming a martyr for someone else's cause. And it was costing me.

There was very little joy and even less relaxation. I was now able to eat all the foods again, but I was still reliant on an osteopath to manage my nervous system.

By almost anyone's standards, I was *made*. But the truth was this: I was the person who was alone, putting on a costume every day for a job I worked at eighty-plus hours a week. The math was bleak: I was spending almost 50 percent of my life in a costume and 30 percent sleeping. And I'm pretty sure the rest of the time was spent exhausted on the couch, watching whatever the latest big show was, and ordering takeout.

I felt a tear drop from my chin to my lap. *This isn't working anymore.*

* * *

There was a point in time when things were particularly tense between my boss and me. To this day, I wonder whether it was the therapy that was at the root of the tension. Perhaps he could sense me craving purpose and fulfillment in something outside of my core responsibilities. Up until therapy came into my life, it was his priorities and the executive priorities that were at the center of everything I did, in every aspect of my life.

Regardless of whether these suspicions were correct or not, at this particular time, the pressure was mounting in the office. There was too much work (even more "too much" than usual) and too few people. None of us were at our best. I personally had gone two years without a vacation (with the exception of a few days over Christmas), as had many others. Even the statutory holidays had been overtaken with emergency calls and demands. I was exhausted and my friend was celebrating his thirtieth birthday over a long weekend in New Orleans.

I hemmed and hawed over the decision to go. We were in the middle of finalizing the plan for a massive project at work.

It's a long weekend. I'm only missing a day and a half of work, I had to remind myself of this over and over again. *I've been on top of this project. It will be fine if I step away for a couple of days.*

And so off I went. For the first time in I couldn't remember how long, I relaxed. I laughed. I had some Hurricane cocktails. I didn't look at my email for thirty-six hours. It worked wonders. I returned from those three days feeling refreshed, rejuvenated, and ready to come back with full energy. My boss's EA came by my desk. "Miles wants to see you right away," she said somewhat sheepishly.

"Right now? But I have—"

"Yeah, right now."

When I walked into his office, he didn't look up or say hello. I walked across the room and sat in my usual chair. He reached across the desk and waved the papers he held in his hand as close to my face as possible. The papers were part of his evidence it turned out—exhibit A—of my downfall from superstar to questionable. I wondered if he was actually going to fire me. "Are you going to tell me that you think it's okay that you're only looking at these now?" The papers bounced in his hand, and his face was taking on a progressively redder hue.

It was Tuesday morning, 8:30 a.m. I'd left for my approved vacation at 3:30 p.m. on Friday. Apparently, he'd left the papers on my chair at 4:30 p.m. on Friday. So I hadn't seen them until this morning. "What I'm saying"—I began, feeling the relaxation of the weekend drain from my body—"is that I wasn't here. I physically wasn't here. I had no way of seeing them!"

"Exactly!" he bellowed, tossing the papers at me. "You weren't here!" I stared down at the papers in my lap and wondered what would have happened had he been holding something bigger, stronger. Would he have thrown that at me too? His eyes had taken on an expression I'd never seen before, and he glared at me as though I were an enemy sent in to break him. He looked ready for war.

I didn't know this man.

His hand dropped to the desk with a thud and his eyes leveled with mine. "There was this time," he said, his voice even and seemingly more controlled. "My son was at this big swim meet. He was set to win, and at the end, I saw him slow down and let another kid win. I thought maybe he had injured himself. But afterward, I asked him about it, and you know what he said? He said, 'Dad, that kid has had a tough year. I've won a lot of medals. So I thought I'd let him win this one.'"

I softened slightly in my chair, wondering where this story of child-hood generosity of spirit was headed. Was this my boss and me? Did he think I was throwing the proverbial race? Or did he want me to let someone else win? He looked out his office window and then back at me. "All that work, all those early mornings, and he lets some other kid win." The red started creeping across his face again, and his eyes took on a glassy finish. "In that moment, I wanted to drown him. I could've just drowned him."

He paused, and just like in a movie, I felt myself gulp, knowing what was about to come next wouldn't be good. "And that's how I feel about you right now. I could drown you, Stephanie. I could just drown you."

* * *

My boss and I had mumbled awkward apologies to each other and decided to chalk up the entire incident to a "dark moment" between us. But I was having a hard time forgetting it, despite the pledged forgiveness.

Were we having a battle of wills? Is that what this was?

I could understand having a reactive outburst, a moment of anger. After all, we'd been working together for close to six years now, an outburst at some point was inevitable. But it felt like a bigger change was happening. I couldn't help feeling stifled these days. It felt like I was constantly biting my tongue. Or asking for permission. It felt like I was giving it all to the organization—everything I had to give—and it never seemed to be enough.

These questions were what I was bringing into therapy with Sonia today. Turns out, it wasn't just grief that you could bring into therapy.

Once I'd updated her, she looked at me with her classic half-smile which always felt like a wink and a "I think you already know the answer to this one, Stephanie."

"How are you doing with your hours these days?" she asked, with a raised eyebrow. "Still working into the night?"

Dammit. She had me there. For months, she'd been pushing me to pull back, maybe focus a little less on the office, and instead, get more in touch with myself. It seemed like advice for people who didn't have pressing deadlines and a big Toronto mortgage to pay for on their own.

It never mattered how I was feeling about my boss. Or about the organization in general, I never pulled back on my hours. I was in the office at 7:45 every morning and still on my computer before going to bed. Work was . . . who I was. It was familiar, comfortable, reliable, needed. And, heck, I was good at it. Really good at it.

"I think it's time to sit in the quiet again and see what comes up," Sonia said.

GETTING CLEAR ON THE COST

To set forth on a personal development journey—and remain committed to that journey through all the ups and downs—usually requires some significant discomfort in your life. When clients come into my coaching practice and talk to me about their coaching goals, their current state, and what they're looking to change, one of my first questions is: *What is the current state costing you?*

The answer to this question—or even the act of asking it—directly influences your personal development journey success. **If you are not feeling a personal cost to the status quo, new actions and new habits will be trickier to take on—and less likely to "stick."** I'd love to sugarcoat that, but in my experience, it's the absolute truth. If you're not feeling like the status quo is in some way untenable for you, there's less impetus for change, and the tough work of personal change will likely not feel worth it to you. And you'll revert to your default behaviors. Understanding the cost of the status quo—and knowing that you are taking active steps to alleviate that "cost"—can be a massive motivator.

I had to miss my dad's moment of death, have my boss threaten to drown me for taking a couple of vacation days, and have my osteopath on speed dial to manage my adrenal system before I really accepted that things needed to change. The cost to my life was becoming undeniable.

Because our core limiting beliefs, personality patterns, and the socially acceptable unconscious productivity loop are such fixtures in our lives, it can be mentally and emotionally easier to stay in the status quo.

Until there's a real cost in your life. Something that feels unsustainable, undesirable, untenable. We often need things to feel really painful—urgent, even—before we're ready to commit to change.

The cost may be *physical*. Maybe your physical health is being compromised by your work. Or perhaps the cost is *emotional*—you are feeling undervalued, underappreciated, or treated in ways that are unacceptable to you.

The cost may be *mental*—you might be feeling ongoing mental disease. Or perhaps the cost is *spiritual*—that is, you feel a lack of inner meaning, inner purpose, or inner alignment.

Or the cost may be a combination of any of the above.

Instead of pushing the costs and discomfort aside (your limiting beliefs, personality patterns, and fear are *great* at rationalizing your current state and talking you out of making changes), take stock of what it is saying to you.

When feeling the discomfort that comes with the cost, it can be tempting to do one of two things: (1) rationalize and return to the status quo, or (2) make a quick (dare I say, hasty) decision in order to escape the discomfort.

Instead, I want you to pause and take stock, so that you can identify and get *conscious* about the underlying issue. There's a great quote from Einstein: "If I had an hour to solve a problem, I'd spend fifty-five minutes thinking about the problem, and five minutes thinking about solutions."

At this point in the process, I want you to spend some time thinking about the problem—"the cost"—that you are facing. The worksheet at the end of this chapter will help you with this.

A NOTE ABOUT FEAR AND RESISTANCE

This is also the point in the process when fear and resistance start to kick in. And when your limiting beliefs and personality constraints shift in to high gear. It's like they can sense that their power over you is waning. You're onto them, and they know it. This can sound like:

Oh, it's not really THAT bad, is it?

Do you REALLY think a change is needed?

It will be just as bad somewhere else. Better the devil you know.

I'll never be able to match this salary again.

When you start getting real about your current state—and what it's costing you—it's as though a switch flips in your brain: *I'm treading into uncertain territory, and I don't like uncertainty. Uncertainty is scary!* Cue to your brain feeding you all kinds of narratives. It can be a real fear-mongerer, that brain of ours.

Know that this is normal. Remind yourself that you aren't making any decisions or changes yet—you are just gathering information. Keep documenting your status quo: What *isn't* working? And what is your current state *costing you*?

In the next chapter, we'll be talking about the *mucky middle*—when the cost is clear, you know things need to change, but those changes feel impossible, daunting, or elusive.

WORKSHEET

TAKE STOCK OF THE COSTS

It's time to take stock of what your current state is *costing* you—physically, emotionally, mentally, and spiritually.

Type of cost	Specific examples and observations	Describe the cost in one sentence
Physical *Impacts to your physical health and body*		
Emotional *How is the status quo contributing to your emotional state?*		
Mental *How is your current state impacting your mental health or creating mental dis-ease?*		
Spiritual *Impacts to integrity, inner purpose, inner meaning, and inner alignment*		

CHAPTER 5

THE MUCKY MIDDLE, OR: *I DON'T KNOW WHAT I WANT, BUT I KNOW IT'S NOT THIS*

It took death, grief, and a heck of a lot of sitting in the quiet for me to realize that I was deeply unsatisfied. That I wanted more for my life, and that my work identity—as it was—wasn't leading me to the life I desired. Only then was I able to say with conviction: *I don't want this anymore. I want something different for my life, and I'm willing to do things differently.* But I still had no idea what or how I needed to change—or what, specifically, I wanted for my life.

MAKING MOVES

During the mucky middle, I played *a lot* of dress-up. I started by going in search of joy: sewing classes, a ballet membership, going to the local theater, exploring new neighborhoods—anything that got me out of my comfort zone of work and into something that truly interested me creatively. I felt myself feeling lighter, brighter.

I started thinking about other career interests: organizational effectiveness, therapy, owning my own Montessori school. I booked conversations and gathered information on every professional thread that interested me. When those seeds of doubt or fear showed up (as they inevitably do) —*Will that pay the bills? You're not trained to do that! Go back to school for another degree, really? Where would the capital come from?*—I jotted them down as future problems to solve and reminded myself that I wasn't making any decisions yet—that I was in the exploratory phase.

And then it happened. One of the professional threads I was exploring completely took hold of me. After the value I'd found in coaching with my executive coach and the therapy I'd had following my dad's death—combined with all the leadership courses, training, and reading I'd done—I found myself reconnecting with my love of psychology and human dynamics.

I signed up for professional coaching training with the Coaches Training Institute and started working my way through their rigorous certification process. I was in love with this work. On my evenings and weekends, I was now working with coaching clients. I put out the call to my network, letting people know I was running a part-time practice, and my roster filled up. Quickly. I was booking 6:30–9:30 p.m., Monday to Thursday—and had a wait list.

- Aspiring entrepreneurs.
- Mid- to senior-level leaders.
- Emerging leaders.
- High performers.
- Big dreamers.

My client list was a dream list.

For the first time in my life, I felt both competent *and* fulfilled. Those three hours every night were joy, no matter how stressful my daytime work life was.

And then the referrals came in, so I added Saturday to my coaching hours.

My coaching clients were happy.

They said I created a safe space for them to talk freely and openly, and they were able to voice dreams, fears, insecurities, and questions in a way they couldn't in any other forum. They felt supported and guided to take action.

And take action they did. I watched them get promoted, start businesses, transform relationships, build teams, land a dream role, and move from self-doubt to self-trust.

Every minute I spent coaching felt purposeful and important. That time one on one with someone looking to evolve, grow, and create fulfillment in their life brought me happiness.

Could there be anything better?

At work, I noticed the same thing. I was the one people came to, to talk things through. My team reported feeling inspired, motivated, and supported. And we pulled off what felt like impossible deadlines. We produced great work. We had fun. And when needed, we had tough conversations.

I became the de facto organizational therapist. And I loved it. I was coaching and developing my team, and listening to, coaching, and advising my colleagues and executives. To the point where I no longer was interested in what was actually described in the title of my role. I found myself coaching people in the office all day, and having to complete my "job responsibilities" in the evenings.

I really loved it: people, teams, and getting real.

There was just one problem. While my job description *did* include people leadership, I was *not* the office therapist. I had budgets to manage, operations to run, steering committees to chair, projects to lead. Which all got in the way of me doing what I now loved most. And where I had the biggest impact.

TAKING STOCK

Here's an interesting fact: I can say with a high degree of certainty that I never would have become a leadership coach without my early career experience. In fact, I'd be willing to bet that I never would have applied for or asked for a leadership role, let alone become a coach.

It was that boss earlier in my career who saw my potential early on. He championed it. He sponsored me. He put me in front of boards and committees. He never once claimed my work as his own. He protected me from attacks from others who were resentful of my climb.

He designed a leadership path for me.

He guided my path; he messaged my path.

He carefully curated every step of that path early on.

He secured funds for my growth.

He went to battle for raises I never asked for.

In those early days, my success was his success. He had given me all of the opportunities I had ever had at that organization. I credit him with all of that.

And for my part, I excelled at achieving whatever he set before me. I worked tirelessly behind the scenes and never rocked the boat or caused any "issues" for him. Perfectly polished, carefully scripted (by myself and him), and always overly prepared. Together, we were wildly successful, a dream team.

Until we weren't.

Until I didn't want to run my speaking notes by him. Every. Single. Time. Until I ditched the overly formal black and gray pantsuits and switched to color. Fuchsia blouses. Patterned skirts. Until I started trusting myself to answer questions in the moment, without burning-the-midnight-oil preparation.

Until my leadership scores came back extremely high.

Until I disagreed with him on how to run a team.

Until I wanted freedom to express myself.

Until I wanted to set my own calendar and take lunches without prior approval.

Until I wanted a personal life and needed to actually use my vacation days.

Until I wanted to define and curate my own leadership style.

Until I was no longer willing to be under anyone's wing and was ready to lead myself.

And that wasn't our deal, our unspoken relationship dynamic. We had grown apart. I was devastated. And terrified. And wildly excited for what would be next. We needed to break up. It wasn't him; it was me.

* * *

You would have thought the path was clear to me, then: I'd found coaching; I was building my practice, I loved it, and my clients were seeing results. The future was obvious, right?

As I look back in hindsight: yep, it sure was.

But my personality patterns and core beliefs weren't done with me yet. I had many more rounds of learning to do before I was ready to accept what I knew to be true for myself. At the time, my truth felt *too* good to be true. And risky. Quit my secure job and become a life and leadership coach full time? What a preposterous idea! But in keeping with what it was costing me, I also knew my current state—the status quo—was no longer an option for me.

I can still remember the day when the phone rang and a prominent individual for whom I had a great deal of respect said bluntly and categorically on the other end of the phone, "I think I have the perfect role for you . . . and I think you're the only one in Canada who can do this well."

Who wouldn't get hooked into those words? I certainly was. I was intrigued, flattered, and hungry for a change, and my next challenge at this particular point in my career. So the conversation quickly became an official job offer. To head up a new endeavor that had a year's worth of start-up funding. My job? Build it from scratch. Essentially operate as a CEO with carte blanche to build. And I had a year to build it to a self-sustaining level.

And so I stepped into a massive leadership role.

ACTION BIAS

When the cost of the status quo is evident to you, and you are aware of the discomfort of it every day—you may be tempted to escape it in just about any way possible.

Action bias is the drive that many of us have to stay busy, stay in action, stay productive. We are conditioned to stay busy and productive. Speed is rewarded in many cases. We bundle projects into fiscal years and business quarters. We are often running from errand to errand, activity to activity. When in the throes of action bias, we don't like to pause; we aren't patient; and we certainly don't like to wait and see, or contemplate. Personally, I am very susceptible to action bias (to my detriment).

Don't get me wrong, action is great and necessary to make changes in our lives. Critical, though, is the timing. *Rushing to action* can have us solving the wrong problem or moving in a direction without conscious thought.

When faced with critical decision points and life changes, taking the time to pause, reflect, and get conscious is critical before moving into action. Otherwise, we can end up in a state that I refer to as life decision whiplash. Feeling a desperation or driving need to get out of our current circumstances, we rush into something that tempts us because, at a surface level, it offers the opposite of our current state. *If my current state isn't fulfilling, then the opposite must be fulfilling, right?* Instead, it becomes life decision whiplash: quickly slamming us into a whole new set of issues to unpack.

Which is exactly what happened to me at this point in the story.

* * *

I had a lot to prove. At least that was the narrative running through my mind every night after I signed on to this new role, heading up a major, new, unproven, ambitious endeavor. I felt scared and out of my element. Could I actually pull this off? I had never held a position with such influence and responsibility as this one.

What was the specific fear? Well, there were several: completely messing it up; publicly failing in a very noticeable way; letting down those who were placing their trust—and their investment—in me to build something that didn't yet exist. The stakes felt very high.

What was underlying *that* fear? My inexperience at having done something similar; something of this scope. That was a fact. *I'd never done anything like this before.*

There were no "rah-rah, you can do it!" positivity mantras that could help. The truth was: I *was* inexperienced. The stakes *were* high. I *could* fail.

So it became an exercise in shifting my mindset in order to face and manage this fear as I pushed the edge of my professional comfort zone and stepped into something completely unfamiliar that was about to challenge me in ways I'd never experienced before.

The options were clear: I could ignore the fear. Push it aside. Put on some bravado. Pretend it didn't exist. Repeat positive affirmations and mantras in the mirror. Fake it until I made it.

Another option was self-sabotage. Call them up and turn down the role. Hide from the new challenge.

The third option—which won out—was to face the fear head on. Not to push it aside, and also not to let fear run the show. In my case, I *was* inexperienced. Did that mean I needed to say no to the role? No. Did it mean I was destined to fail in the role? No. Did it mean I needed to unpack the fear and take stock of my areas of inexperience and build those skill sets? Absolutely.

So, in that moment of fear, when the thought of public failure and letting everyone down was sweeping over me in the days and weeks before I stepped into the position, it became critical to take stock of the fear. And so I took inventory by breaking down the role into its varied parts, ranking myself on where I felt I had stronger versus weaker or limited experience and skill.

I spoke to others in similar roles to find out what they wished they'd done differently in their first year of leadership—mistakes they'd made, challenges they'd faced. I documented their insight and thought about how I might handle those same issues.

I devised a plan to build my knowledge and skill in the areas where

I was weaker, and a list of individuals I could reach out to for support and insight in those areas until I felt I had built my competence.

I was ready.

* * *

I had overridden the initial fear narrative. I had stepped into the role, mapped out a development plan for myself, and sought out expertise as needed. But the demands of the role began to consume me quickly.

Some fun facts about this venture:

Funding had yet to be determined.

The communities and organizations to be served—the beneficiaries—had yet to be defined.

A staffing plan was nonexistent.

Partnerships were yet to be secured.

We had been gifted funding for a year to give us runway to become self-sustaining, self-funded.

Did I have massive supporters as I stepped into this role? Absolutely. Did I also have really staunch critics? You betcha.

I was stepping into the intersection of many fields of expertise: academia, health care, finance, and government policy. I didn't know any one person who had depth of expertise across all four of those areas, and yet here I was stepping into a role that required deep understanding and expertise across all of them. The mission was exciting, exhilarating, and inspiring. But the execution often felt impossible.

There were people who wanted me to fail and were explicit about it. I had individuals who refused to acknowledge my presence in rooms because I didn't hold a PhD.

There were people who wanted me to fail who hid it well. Smiling and shaking my hand in congratulations and motherhood statements of support, who whispered skepticism behind the scenes or never followed through on promises.

There were those who saw an opportunity for a power play and attached themselves to what they thought might be a winning ticket. Their support was always tenuous and conditional. I was always one perceived misstep away from losing their support.

And there were people who were so unbelievably and unwaveringly kind, supportive, and walked through it with me the whole way.

Never had there been such a swirl of competing, hostile, and supportive external forces all looking to define where I was to place my focus and how I was to go about accomplishing those goals. Or to erode and undermine my progress.

The learning curve for this role had me up all hours of the night reading, learning, and poring over documents.

The demands from the varied stakeholders were both valid and relentless and swirled through my mind all hours of the day.

The to-do list grew. All my years of being diligent about setting priorities and identifying what was essential were challenged. There simply wasn't enough person-power or people resources to do every-thing that needed to be done. Many very critical things were essential. And despite ongoing and significant support from the donors and advisors, I was the only one who was solely dedicated to the venture.

And so I took it all on. It was exhilarating and daunting all at once. We began to build momentum. Day in and day out, there was just me to ideate, deliver, manage, and create. I was both tired and energized, believing fully that this work would make a difference, that every drop of mental, physical, and emotional energy I was pouring into it was worth it.

After all, I was the one setting the pace. It was my decision to work the long hours, to invest the time.

I was certain that THIS—this new freedom, autonomy, and bigger leadership scope—was what had been missing all those years. I was sure of it. The whispers that had come to me years ago when I had sat in the quiet were making sense now. *This* is what they wanted for me, a bigger leadership role, a bigger platform, autonomy over my calendar, and freedom to use my voice.

And as months went by, I built awareness, pounded the proverbial pavement, enlisted donors, and hosted events. Day by day, the word was spreading. We weren't going away. We started to gather new supporters—new voices and perspectives—with new interests and often competing demands.

* * *

Everything ramped up as we moved through our 365 days and goal of sustainable funding.

I was bleary eyed and exhausted by day 225. I kept telling myself: *Once we pass the year, things will settle down. We just need the funding lined up.*

Emails came in by the hundreds every hour. New requests, new opportunities. My advisors, who were always generous and helpful, were also sources of unrelenting demands and opportunities, which was necessary in those early days. We were all trying to secure what was needed.

But I remained the only one on the ground, able to implement quickly.

Within the span of an evening, I would be committed to three research projects, two radio interviews, four funding applications, and seven donor leads. The wheel was spinning successfully. Almost too successfully. At 11 p.m., my head pounded as I took in the new requests.

Did I raise an alarm bell? Of course not. Instead, I sent a series of email responses saying variations of the following:

Of course I can!

Sounds good!

Great opportunity!

The interviews sound fantastic!

I'll get on those funding applications!

Each response filled with exclamation points, enthusiasm, and "let's do this!"

I poured myself another cup of coffee, bracing for another late night. All the while my head was throbbing.

My index and middle fingers pressed into my temples on both sides, and I began pushing them in and around in small circles.

That voice inside my head: *We're over-committing. We're taking on too much. We can't do it all well. We need to pace. Pause.*

But I stayed silent.

They were securing opportunities, and we needed opportunities.

They were counting on me to take these opportunities and build.

And so I worked.

And emailed.

And called.

And wrote.

Eighteen hours a day, every day. We only had 140 days left.

The words on the screen were becoming blurry. My phone displayed missed calls from my family, my friends. My heart was racing, while my mind wanted to pull a blanket up over my head and sleep for a year.

An email flashed across the screen from one of the advisors. Subject line: MERGER!

A not-so-funny and familiar thing started happening to me again—my body started rejecting food. Everything but saltine crackers with a thin spread of butter. It was similar to back in the day when I rejected everything but boiled potatoes.

I sat in my doctor's office, demanding a fix.

"You need to rest," she said sternly.

"I'm moderating a filmed industry event in four days. I don't need rest; I need something that will give me back my appetite and my energy." I pushed back. I didn't have time for sleep or rest or vacations. We had 140 days to go. We were so close. *I* was so close. Besides, my advisors didn't *rest*. Neither would I.

From my perch on the examining table, I could hear the ding of my phone as new emails and missed calls came in. With each *ding* I felt my stomach flop.

I stomped out of the doctor's office, ignoring and irritated by her warnings. She just didn't get it. I was busy building something. Too busy for rest, too busy for down time, and certainly too busy to slow down.

* * *

Before the front hallway mirror at 6:30 a.m., the dread washed over me. The image reflecting back at me was blondish-brown hair pulled back in a low bun with bangs falling in a perfect line just under my eyebrows and stiffened with enough hairspray to ensure they would remain unchanged from the time I arrived at the 7 a.m. breakfast meeting that morning until the "Women in Finance" event wrapped up later that night at nine. My makeup, which consisted of many shades of neutral (which I'm pretty sure was labeled "the corporate collection" at Sephora), was bookended by silver stud earrings. A three-string necklace of pearls and silver chains clung to the top of my tailored gray knee-length dress, which draped over sheer pantyhose. Anchoring the look were my three-inch all-day-comfort-yet-look-uncomfortable (a look which came with an exorbitantly expensive price tag) black patent leather heels. A fitted black cardigan draped over my left forearm (ready to go on once I exited the subway to ensure I was never showing too much skin within a 100-foot radius of the office) extended out to my palm, which cradled my phone. My right shoulder was raised up and tensed slightly under the weight of the computer bag strap digging in.

This was the female financial executive uniform. This was my world. Every day, you'd find thousands of us clicking through Toronto's underground PATH system as we closed deals, met clients, wooed new ones, or raced for a ten-minute grab-and-dash-back-to-the-desk lunch, with a twelve-hour work day often considered a good, balanced one. The underground PATH—equally beloved and loathed—connected the banks, pension funds, consulting firms, insurance companies, and law firms by a series of shopping tunnels lined with every service, store, and caffeinated product you could ever want or need. It ensured that you never had a reason to leave the financial network and never remembered that the sun shone on weekdays as well. It was designed with one thing in mind: keep the hamsters scurrying about the web of concrete towers, earning, generating, promising, transferring, and securing money.

This was not the first morning I'd felt unease and dread wash over me. I felt it often when a work crisis hit or an 11 p.m. email came in that had to be dealt with before the morning or when a deadline was arbitrarily brought forward by two weeks. This time, though, was different. There was no crisis, no late-night email, no deadline. In fact, it had been a relatively straightforward week at the office. This dread and unease was something different entirely. It stemmed from this inner voice that—if I let myself sit in silence long enough—spoke very kindly, but firmly: *This is not who you are.*

Staring again at my reflection, I wondered if I was having an out-of-body experience. It was me observing me. Observing the absurdity of this woman dressed in this costume and how she was spending her days. Suddenly I was back in my university business class. Here I stood, just one of the many would-be financial executives playing dress-up and showing up every day to move money through the system.

* * *

Then, finally, came the day my body had had enough. I was lying on the couch, eyes closed. The screen had become a blur hours ago, the typed sentences started to scramble and blend together. It was so warm and cozy under the blanket I'd swaddled myself into.

Words, as they came into my mind, sounded ridiculous. I let the word "proposal" swim and somersault through my mind and over my tongue. It sounded nonsensical and unknown.

I couldn't remember why we were writing this latest proposal.

From the couch, I reached for my coffee, but as I sipped it, it tasted foreign. I felt my face frown as I placed the mug back on the coffee table and pushed it out of arm's reach.

My eyes flitted, my eyelids pulled down like a heavy velvet theatre curtain signaling the very end of the performance.

What was happening to me?

I was so tired. The thought of placing a foot on the floor and walking to the kitchen felt impossible. It was as though over a year of tiredness had ganged up on me. That tidal wave of tiredness had flattened me to this couch. I tried thrashing around, tried fighting it, tried resisting it. But I remained flattened.

I had no choice, it seemed, but to surrender completely.

The vibration of my phone against the glass of the coffee table interrupted the haze long enough for me to catch the name flashing across the screen.

Mumbling something incomprehensible even to myself, I reached out from under the blanket with a desire to toss the phone to the ground, but succeeded only in poking it, pushing it into the untouched glass of water from the night before.

The movement, combined with the glare of daylight pushing through the closed slats of my living room shutters, sent a bolt of pain from behind my left eye through to the far corner of my mind, where it landed as an unshakable dull ache. I yanked at the blanket—it and I both unmoved and unchanged for twenty-four hours—and pulled it up and over my head, allowing myself to sink into the dark corner of the couch that had become my refuge.

I couldn't talk to anyone. Not now. Not like this. *Truly dedicated people don't go down—they power through.* I felt like an exhausted failure.

I took a big gulp of water and immediately regretted it. The gulp was too much for my stomach, a stomach that had struggled to keep medication, let alone food and water, down for two weeks. I rolled over and pulled the bucket to my mouth and threw up the gulp I'd just swigged down.

The new message notification ding of the phone reverberated through the room.

I closed my eyes again and put my hand to my forehead to rub the ache. Another gulp of water down, another gulp lost. And the cycle continued.

My get-up-and-go had got up and left.

And while I wasn't fully lucid, I could feel something deep within me stir, and it wasn't the fever. My life, as it was, was making me ill. In that swaddle, on that couch, with that email in hand, I was scared, and oh so desperately sad. I felt caught in a web, and it seemed that every move I made either entangled me further or enabled the next strand to be woven, enabled the web to grow stronger, bigger. I wanted to fall ever so softly and ever so unnoticed from the web.

Something's got to give.

Dad's face flitted through my mind then, and I made an attempt to punch the throw cushion in front of me. I covered my face with my hands, exhausted, ashamed.

I've failed, Dad. I don't know how to make this work. I've let every-one down, and I don't know what to do.

And just like that, the world went dark, and I fell into the blankets, fevered and chronically dehydrated.

* * *

I might have escaped the discomfort of my previous role, but I'd managed to hurl myself—along with all of my limiting beliefs and personality constraints—directly into a pressure cooker and turned the dial to high.

My lifestyle was now worse than it had been before. Any semblance of balance I'd had prior had now been completely eviscerated.

It was classic life decision whiplash.

My inner knowing had been very clear: life and leadership coaching lit me up. Only months prior, I had a wait list for my part-time practice. I had now abandoned that practice to build this new venture—attaching even more firmly to all of my oh-so-familiar limiting beliefs and spinning in the unconscious productivity loop at an even greater speed. Now I had *more* external validators and goals, *more* comparison, *more* hustle.

I was no longer coaching. I was back in hyper-productivity, running myself ragged to deliver on others' demands and needs, and to honor the responsibilities I had signed up for. **And—a very important point to underline—*I had signed up for this.*** I was accountable. It was not the fault of the role or the advisors. I was the one that had allowed myself to move so far away from my own truth.

At this point in the story, I was still battling with my beliefs around productivity. I continued to be rewarded for my work ethic, productivity, and ability to succeed. I was tracking toward the 365-day goal.

All while maintaining relationships. All with a smile on my face, even if it was an exhausted one. To the outside world, I still presented as a success. And that was still critically important to me.

But I was still failing on the inside, because I was abandoning myself. I was exhausted and unfulfilled. I was working because that's what I did: there was a goal that someone had declared, and I was the person designated to achieve it. And so I did. And so is it any surprise that the same costs showed up?

I was still single.

I wasn't able to socialize with my friends.

My health was compromised.

I lived in a permanent state of stress.

I wasn't able to enjoy my success—or my life.

I found myself in even greater misery. More confused and unfulfilled than ever. I was in the muck.

How had this happened? And more importantly, what was I supposed to do now?

I was still hooked into *external* success measures and still succumbing to my Enneagram Type 9 vice of *self-forgetting*. I was still operating almost entirely *unconsciously*. Except that I'd had a glimmer of conscious productivity: my coaching practice. While it still felt like an impractical pipe dream, the dream was there—floating in the back of my mind, delicate and flimsy, waiting for me to give it shape.

TIME FOR SOME NEW BELIEFS

At this point, I still wasn't sure what it even meant to feel fulfilled in my life. But I was certainly starting to understand what deep unfulfillment felt like. My limiting belief that fun, rest, and joy needed to be earned was further constricting my life.

Through all of it—the demands, the challenges, the stress—there was a stubbornness in me as well. I wanted to believe I could do it all. That no request was too much. That "no" wasn't an appropriate response. It didn't matter how many people raised their eyebrows or shook their heads when they heard of my work life. "How exactly are you managing all of this work?" they would ask.

I wore it as a badge of honor that I was managing all that work. I wanted to prove all of those raised eyebrows wrong. Because it felt like a taunt, like a personal slight, a dare, as though they were questioning my ability and capability, my very being. When I heard them ask that question, what I heard was an emphasis on "you" and not on "all this work," as though they were skeptical of my abilities. That others wouldn't have an issue managing all of this work; that the problem was me. They doubted ME in this role. And the only way to prove them wrong and to demonstrate my talent was to get all the work done. Without complaint. Without exhaustion.

Do you see how I was still cycling in the *unconscious productivity* loop? Externally identified goals and extreme hustle in service of those goals. Desperation to prove myself to others and be validated. The truth was: I still felt most valuable when I worked. Worth and work were still synonymous for me.

And in classic Enneagram Type 9 *self-forgetting* style, I let myself believe it was possible to never stop. And to get it all done. Ignoring my needs, my health, and my personal life. And in this particular case of this role, I was surrounded by advisors with their own limiting beliefs, and personality constraints. We were a pack of overachieving dreamers, none of whom wanted to be the negative one. All of whom wanted to be a contributor and to be the one to lay claim to the latest great idea to move us forward.

Our respective limiting beliefs and personality constraints were running the show.

And here we were, drowning in commitments. And me, at the helm with adrenal issues I had refused to acknowledge.

I was burned out.

I'd hit a new low point, and the only thing that could save me now was a whole new set of beliefs. It was time to shed those familiar limiting beliefs I'd had my whole life and trade them in for some new ones that would actually serve me. And that's precisely where we're headed next in Chapter 6.

REFLECTION

LIFE DECISION WHIPLASH

Life decision whiplash happens when the discomfort of one situation has you making a quick decision to change your circumstances. The speed of the decision leaves little to no time for reflection, and as a result, you find yourself in a situation that is no better—perhaps worse—than the one you left.

Questions for you to consider:

- When have you experienced life decision whiplash?

- What did you learn about yourself as a result?

- How will that inform your next big life decision?

WORKSHEET

YOUR POSSIBILITY GENERATOR

- What do you want *more* of in your life?

- What do you want *less* of?

- What have you not allowed yourself to consider possible?

- What limiting belief are you ready to shed?

CHAPTER 6

DECISION POINT: THE OFF-RAMP

I was in an emotional state I'd never encountered before. It was definitely a low point—one of the lowest of my life—but it was compounded by uncertainty, confusion, and terror. If I'm being really honest, there was a feeling of despair mixed in as well. Something in me knew I couldn't go back to the way things were; but at the same time, I had no idea how to do things differently.

To this day, low points and hard emotions scare me. I will still catch myself trying to avoid sitting in the discomfort of a tough emotion. In the past, when I would get close to something sad, depressing, dark, or scary, suddenly I'd try to lighten the mood or brush off the topic. This is often true with my clients too.

Here's what I've come to learn, though, having sat through my fair share of low points: they are the throughway to joy. I promise. Remember that saying "the only way out is through"? I believe that to be one of the truest statements ever to be uttered. Sure, you can go your whole life avoiding something you'd rather not face, but you'll never get to true joy and fulfillment without understanding *why* that something is so hard to face and working your way through it.

For me, at this particular point in time in my life, my low point was of my own making: I was working endlessly at a pace and intensity that left no space for other areas of life. My limiting beliefs—which led to workaholism and productivity addiction—made me very successful and also very miserable and depleted.

And why did I keep repeating these patterns over and over again? Because of my limiting beliefs, my personality constraints, and a fear of facing my own inner truth.

We will keep spinning and repeating the same patterns unless we *interrupt* our limiting beliefs, personality constraints, and tune in to our inner truth. This interruption is what I call *the off-ramp, a*nd it's a critical point if we hope to move from *unconscious* to *conscious productivity.*

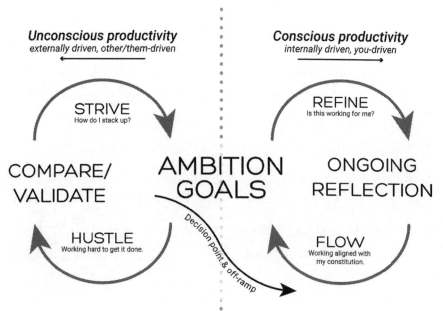

Let's revisit the journey from unconscious productivity to conscious productivity (refer to image on page 164).

The *off-ramp* is the point at which we start to move from *unconscious productivity* (and being driven by *external* drivers) to *conscious productivity* (and being driven by our own *internal knowing*).

THE DECISION TO MOVE FROM UNCONSCIOUS TO CONSCIOUS PRODUCTIVITY

The key to successfully navigating the off-ramp and moving from unconscious productivity to conscious productivity is this: recognize your limiting beliefs for what they are (both "limiting" and "beliefs" that can be changed) and *experiment with new beliefs anchored in your own inner truth.*

Conscious productivity is also grounded in self-trust: trusting yourself to challenge what isn't working, trusting yourself to take action in service of new beliefs, and trusting yourself to reflect on that action and make adjustments as needed. *This* is conscious productivity. You won't hit optimal fulfillment the first time, every time, but you're committed to approaching your life with conscious intention.

When you start to make reflection a practice, you can't unlearn what you've experienced, and it's much harder to ignore your own inner compass once you are in regular connection with it. You'll notice that it usually has a clear answer—it just may be one that feels challenging to implement.

In my case, my inner compass was telling me that I needed to slow my pace, pay some attention to my personal life, and maybe—just maybe—inject some joy and play into my life. That, perhaps, work wasn't the entirety of my identity.

I needed to start saying no to others—and yes to myself.

* * *

I could now tolerate coffee. Black coffee. I'd been on the couch for more than two weeks, with very little memory of what had transpired. I'd lost fourteen pounds during that time. My neighbor, who had a key to my place, had apparently seen me through the window and had dropped off ginger ale at some point.

My laptop lay dormant and unused in the far-left corner of the bed. One flick of my foot would have nudged it right off the covers and out of eyesight. My phone was within arm's reach. I could stretch my right arm out just enough to catch the phone's edge between my fingertips. But I didn't nudge the computer or grasp for the phone.

For the first time in years, possibly ever, I just lay there at 4:30 in the afternoon on a Tuesday with:

The to-do list unchecked.
The computer in sleep mode.
The phone on silent.
Briefing documents and deliverables approaching their due dates.
Hundreds of unread emails.

I lay there under the covers and stared at the slanted ceiling above me. The sun pushed through the window shutter slats, resting on my outstretched hands and feet.

I exhaled. I inhaled. Eyes closed. Eyes opened.

Work was left undone. This was less of a choice and more a matter of my mind being unable to take in the words on the screen and an unwillingness of my fingers to race across a keyboard. My usually sunny and optimistic disposition was replaced by a low hanging, dense fog.

Given what I now know about burnout and severe exhaustion, this wasn't surprising. The executive functioning of the brain is compromised when we're in this state resulting in fogginess, an inability to connect the dots between ideas, poor attention and memory, and an inability to focus. Check, check, check, check.

I was becoming someone I didn't like. My life was becoming a string of unfulfilling demands.

Was I just not cut out for this work world?
I wasn't the first one to work long hours or to be caught up in stressful deadlines.
Was I just too weak?
Was I not ambitious or tough enough?

My eyes remained on the ceiling, and I continued to just lie there, doing nothing, letting the questions and the confusion and the exhaustion circle through me.

Oddly enough, despite the exhaustion, despite the lack of fulfill-ment, I still felt a compulsion to check my email. To write a to-do list. Otherwise, now that I was conscious and feeling a bit stronger, what was I to do for the rest of the day? If not work, then what?

As my eyes narrowed in on a patch of ceiling, the question morphed into a much bigger one, and my stomach lurched: Who am I, if not my work? And if I am my work, why is it rendering me unconscious and exhausted in my bed?

And then I was struck with the same lament as after Dad died and I'd sat in the quiet all those years ago.

What am I doing with my life?

All of these years, all of this work, what was it all for?

Like a video montage, the scenes flashed across the big screen of my mind . . . running home with my report cards, extra credit work, early acceptance to business school, ongoing straight A's, the corpor-ate climb at work. I'd been taught to strive, to celebrate ambition. I'd been conditioned to power ahead.

What does it really mean to be ambitious? What if I slowed down, did less? Would I still be worthy then? I couldn't answer that question with certainty, because I'd never tested it. I'd never slowed down, never stopped achieving, never stopped performing.

This was truth. The ambition, the striving, the career choices. It was all a hustle for worth, for acceptance. I could hear the continuous hum of cars driving by outside the window, while my eyes stayed glued on that patch of ceiling.

What, or who, the heck am I doing this for?

* * *

I eventually left my bedroom, but the fog remained. I felt disconnected from joy, from fulfillment, and wasn't sure I had any idea how to have fun and create ease in my life.

And I'd come to realize this low point was of my own making: I was working endlessly on work that was misaligned with my purpose and true talents. I was working at a pace and intensity that left no space for other areas of life. Workaholism and productivity addiction made me very successful—and also very miserable and depleted.

I can still feel myself lying on the bed and the realization crashing down on me with a thud: the way I was living my life just wasn't working.

I had to make some changes.

Through the night, I'd fantasized about resigning. But quitting was risky. I had bills—including a giant mortgage—to pay. This created a frantic loop in my mind: stay, continue to burn out, and be financially secure *or* leave, feel fulfilled, and lose my house.

I was stuck in either/or thinking. Forcing myself to choose between two undesirable options.

As I continued to rest, though, I found my thought process changing. Instead of remaining fixed on these two undesirable outcomes, I started exploring *what else* might be possible.

Maybe, just maybe, there was a middle ground. What if I didn't quit, but simply scaled back?

What if I decided not to work twelve-plus hour days?

What if they became eight-hour days instead, with longer hours only as absolutely needed?

What if I said no to evening calls if they conflicted with the Pilates class I'd been talking about attending for years?

What if I closed my computer and made it to Thursday night beach volleyball with my neighbors for once?

What if I sat outside, right here on my very own terrace, for thirty minutes every day at lunch—without my phone?

And then the most controversial of questions came to the fore—what if, instead of prioritizing work for this summer, I prioritized fun instead?

With every "what if," my spine straightened, my gaze shifted to the sky, and my leaden heart softened. It felt revelatory.

What if I committed to a scale back—a *BIG* scale back?

The idea had me feeling like a child rolling down a grassy hill in the summer—gathering momentum and full of joy.

I jumped from the sofa with a zip I hadn't felt in months and hurried inside to my journal, turning to a new page. At the top I penned "The Big Scale Back" and underneath that heading, I scribbled four things:

Have fun.

Pay the bills.

Move my body.

Love.

These four things. These were to be my new measures of success.

I read and reread that list, my smile stretching its corners each time. It felt radical. And given the nature of my work and the people involved, it also felt risky.

I was living in a business world where 24/7 email was the norm, where being busy was celebrated, and not sleeping was often a sign of an impending promotion. These fantasies of mine—of lunches outside, saying no to evening calls and emails—how would they be received?

Could I go against these not-so-unspoken corporate rules and succeed?

Could I flip my entire approach to work and life upside down?

Could I find balance, peace, and ease and still pay the bills?

There was only one way to find out: I'd put it into practice. Starting tomorrow.

I had absolutely no way of knowing the end game. I felt both gleeful and terrified.

And so the big scale back began.

* * *

It felt bizarre at first. To wake up and *not* look at my phone. As part of the scale back, I'd declared a new routine: all devices were left in my home office as of 8 p.m. I went back to an old-school clock in my bedroom, rather than using my phone as a clock and alarm.

Once I woke up, I'd make myself coffee and a smoothie and head to my terrace. No checking my phone, no email, no distractions. Just me, my multiple beverages, and the terrace. At first, this routine led to a mild panic every morning. Thoughts began cycling through my mind:

What if I'd been sent an urgent message in the night?

What if I was forgetting a meeting this morning?

I closed my eyes, breathed deeply and pushed the thoughts aside and let myself sink into my outdoor sofa. It was 7 a.m.

I am giving myself thirty minutes. There is no urgent email or meeting between 7:00 and 7:30 a.m.

But, wow, did my underlying belief system put up a fight at first. Trying to convince me I was about to drop the ball, that I would get fired, that I was a lazy human being.

But in time, that thirty minutes became sixty minutes, which eventually became ninety. On the terrace, in full sun, I sunk back on the outdoor sofa cushions and let the sun's rays touch down on my alabaster skin. Skin that had been draped in dress shirts and cardigans for as many hot sunny July days as I could remember. So many vacation days left untaken, as business initiatives took priority.

Every morning from 7:00 to 8:30 became sacred time for me, to do whatever felt right for me in the moment.

Over time, I felt the tension melting, as though my body were singing its gratitude: *Yes*, it seemed to be saying. *This.*

Fifteen years of grasping, gripping, striving, proving were slowly being drawn from me, like vapor evaporating in the heat.

Let go, let go of it all.

One morning, one of my fears materialized: I dropped into a

cavernous deep sleep out there on the terrace. It felt like the sleep of a warrior leaving the battlefield exhausted, victorious, and bones bursting with the delight of returning home. I awoke on the terrace hours later, as a butterfly lifted up and off the arm of the sofa. As my eyes blinked awake and I took in my surroundings, I felt different. I felt . . . rested. Deeply, thoroughly rested.

And the world hadn't fallen apart while I slept.

The questions about my life, myself, my career, were still circling and dancing through my mind. I still didn't have answers to any of them. But feeling rested certainly felt like a start.

Maybe rest is the answer.

EXPERIMENTING WITH NEW BELIEFS

Let's revisit the key to successfully navigating the off-ramp and moving from unconscious productivity to conscious productivity: recognize your limiting beliefs for what they are (both "limiting" and "beliefs" that can be changed), *and experiment with new beliefs anchored in your own inner truth.*

For me, the thought of scaling back my hours and taking lunch breaks in the sun felt completely revolutionary. Why? Because those actions smacked right up against my limiting beliefs. I thought joy, rest, and socializing had to be earned—only a possibility when the to-do list was complete. And yet, the to-do lists would *never* be complete.

Declaring the scale back was me declaring a possible set of *new beliefs:*

Joy, rest, and socializing don't need to be earned.

I am more than my work.

My definition of success includes my health and happiness.

I also consciously chose to keep the positive elements of my previous belief structure: work ethic and responsibility. It was important for me to honor my responsibilities, pay the bills, and contribute to successful outcomes in my work.

Declaring new beliefs doesn't mean abandoning *everything* about your previous beliefs. It's about switching your belief structure from *unconscious* to *conscious*—and from *limiting* to *serving*. You are in the driver's seat.

Looking back on my work experiences, there were times when work felt easy (not necessarily a good thing) and times when it felt hard (not necessarily a bad thing); times when it energized me (more of that work, please), and when it depleted me (important information to take note of). I remember feeling highly fulfilled at times as well as highly under- and wrongly utilized (sometimes at the same organization). I'd worked in environments and workplaces that were inspiring and innovative, as well as ones that bred toxicity and fear.

I'd had colleagues and leaders who pushed my buttons in great ways, ways that helped me to grow and evolve. I'd had others who behaved in ways that were out of alignment with my values and ultimately led to me making the decision to leave the organization.

Throughout all of these circumstances and environments, one thing was constant: *me*. I chose each and every one of those roles and workplaces. I chose the boundaries I set. I chose how to live into my values every day. I'm always reminded of that quote by Jon Kabat-Zinn: "Everywhere you go, there you are."

If I wanted to change my life circumstances, I needed to change the way I showed up in my life. I had to consciously choose my beliefs, and how I put those beliefs into practice every day. I needed to give myself permission (and garner up the courage) to do things my own way. In a way that honored my own desires, my own constitution, and my own gifts and talents.

The same applies to you: **to change your life circumstances, you need to _consciously_ choose your beliefs and how you put those beliefs into practice every day.** You don't need to have the same beliefs or goals as anyone else. Or if you do, you don't have to go about living into those beliefs—or achieving those goals—the same way others do. YOU are the expert in YOU. Grant yourself full permission to do it in your own way, honoring your own desires, your own constitution, and your own gifts and talents.

TAPPING INTO YOUR OWN INNER KNOWING

Societal and external expectations—combined with our limiting beliefs and personality constraints—create a lot of mental and emotional "noise." This noise can be so loud that it can completely block us from our own inner knowing.

Your inner wisdom, your intuition, knows what's best—yet external expectations, limiting beliefs, and personality constraints will put up barriers, excuses, and rationalizations. Intuition hasn't always received the respect it deserves. I know I grew up valuing logic and analysis over anything that would be considered "inner knowing." Logic and data felt safer because I certainly didn't trust myself, and often my inner whisperings directly contradicted what everyone around me thought was the "right" or "best" thing to do. And so I tuned it out. Remember when I pushed aside creative writing for math, humanities for business, and rest in order to power through? And just about every whisper that came to me when I sat in the quiet?

My inner knowing always knew what was right for me. It just didn't align with what I'd been conditioned to believe was right. While intuition and gut feelings were once considered pseudoscience, studies have since shown scientific evidence for intuition. Quite powerful evidence, in fact. *Harvard Business Review*, among other reputable business sources, has written about this research and its importance—when to leverage intuition for decision-making and when not to. When it comes to intuition, what jumps out in the literature is the connection between intuition and expertise.

The more expertise we have in a specific area—that is, we've spent a lot of time focused on that topic and experienced it in a number of situations and settings—the more beneficial it can be to trust our intuition or gut feeling when making a decision, rather than data and analytics. This may raise the question: *Geez, I'm not an expert in that many things, so should I not trust my intuition?*

Here's my take: we are all experts in *ourselves*. You are the expert in *you*. So when it comes to decisions about what makes the most sense for *you* from a career perspective, a relationship perspective, or goal perspective, I believe intuition and gut feeling is your *best* guidepost when making these decisions. You have experienced yourself since childhood. You know how you feel across numerous situations. You've been with yourself through the ups and downs, and you know what your inner voice whispers to you in the wee hours of the night or when you sit alone with your thoughts.

Your conditioning, your beliefs—everything discussed in the first half of this book—may have you *override* what you know or *talk you out* of what you know. But if you can stand firm in challenging your unconscious beliefs (that are now becoming conscious!) and really listen to what comes up when you sit in the quiet, you will know what you truly want for yourself and your life. You'll know what needs to change.

You *can* and *will* change your life experience, if you choose.

At this point in the process, I want you to consciously "try on" some new beliefs that challenge your status quo. Check in with yourself—and your own inner knowing—to determine what new beliefs might best serve you, and what you're most desiring for your life. The worksheets on the following pages will support you in doing this. It's one thing to declare it; it's another to turn it into a new way of living. In the next chapter, we'll look at *how* to design your life around your new beliefs and desired state.

PRACTICE

SIT IN NATURE

What you'll need: a notebook or journal, a writing utensil, a spot in nature, and an hour of uninterrupted time.

Find a spot—ideally in nature if you can—where you can sit or walk peacefully by yourself. Give yourself plenty of time (when you aren't in a rush or time bound). Ideally, I suggest giving yourself at least an hour. Let your mind wander, and let yourself take in your surroundings. Look at whatever nature has to offer around you.

Then, jot down your thoughts in response to the following questions:

- What's working really well in my life right now?

- What's not working well?

- What would I like to change?

- What am I desiring most?

WORKSHEET

IDENTIFY NEW BELIEFS

Think back to the limiting beliefs that you identified in Chapter 1 and the costs you identified in Chapter 4.

What parts of your belief structure would you like to challenge?

What parts of your belief structure would you like to maintain?

What new beliefs would you like to "try on"?

What actions—big or small—will help you to "try on" these new beliefs?

WORKSHEET

An important note: Getting conscious and declaring what you really want can bring up a lot. A lot. It starts to get real. Your ego resists, fear might set in, and excuses might shower over you. So at this point, if that is starting to happen, I want you to pause and tell yourself that identifying the changes and declaring what you want for yourself doesn't mean you're taking full action . . . yet. For now, simply let yourself declare what it is you most desire—without any pressure to make any changes. And if you need or want to, keep it really simple: imagine what your ideal Tuesday, or work week, might look like.

CHAPTER 7

CLARITY, COMMITMENT, AND CURATION

Welcome to conscious productivity, where you are going to take everything that you've taken stock of in the first half of this book and now start to consolidate it. The entire purpose of conscious productivity is to design your life deliberately and on purpose, setting up the mindset, practices, boundaries, and habits that support it.

You've taken the off-ramp. You're stepping into a possible future. You consciously recognize your limiting beliefs and your personality constraints that have influenced your goals and aspirations in the past—and you're making a conscious effort to question them, create new beliefs, and try on different ways of showing up in the world.

As you do, what are you learning about yourself? About your relationship with work and the rest of your life? Your end state may still be a little fuzzy, but you're starting to feel your way into a different way of living.

Maybe you're starting to get some pushback as you try on your new beliefs, and show up in a different way. This pushback may be coming from yourself or from those around you. In this chapter, you'll learn how to execute this new vision for your life in a way that is sustainable and true to yourself.

* * *

I remember my Grade 8 year passing quickly. My clique of four girls would be disbanded come September, each of us headed to a different high school. We stood huddled together with our families on graduation night, snapping photos. Tucked under my arms were both the French and English awards for outstanding performance. My parents lined me up against the school wall, positioned one award in each hand, and encouraged me to hold them up for the photo. I agreed, but only if it could be taken in a hallway around the corner from all the activity. I'd managed to keep most of my grades and performance well hidden, and in doing so, had escaped being labeled a full-out nerd—or worse, a loser. And so we snuck around the corner, took the photo, and returned to the reception in the lunchroom with everyone else.

Some of my classmates were crying, others were taking turns signing yearbooks, some were talking about what they'd get up to in high school. "You can leave the school at lunch and get PIZZA!" I heard Jeff yell from across the room.

All I felt in that moment was relief. Relief to be done performing for these particular teachers; to be done hiding test results and uttering "I can't remember" when asked what my grade was in a particular course, fearful that doing well in school would make me a social pariah. I'd seen it happen to Tracy. She'd busied herself away at recess, cramming for tests, and would declare her results with a boldness that our insecure 11- and 12-year-old selves took as blatant over-confidence. "She thinks she's better than everyone else," the other girls would whisper. "What a loser."

They'd giggle, the boys around them would giggle, and just like that, the rules of social engagement in our classroom were set. Don't be more successful than anyone else, or if you are, keep your success to yourself. And so I had. Silently earning high marks in every class, and going completely unnoticed. Hiding, and maintaining this facade, was exhausting.

And so graduation marked a certain freedom. I had no idea who my teachers would be in high school or what my classroom would be like. No idea about the coursework. The next few months could be spent however I chose.

The next day, the sun shone brightly. Dad was off golfing; Mum and Sherryl were running errands. I took my Discman and journal to the backyard of my childhood home. I lay down in the grass next to the wooden swing set. Alone, and without pressures of any kind, I pressed "play" and my ears filled with the sound of Pearl Jam halfway through "Alive."

As "Alive" came to an end and "Why Go" began, I sunk deeper into the grass. With no one home, our backyard felt like my own estate. My pencil and notebook lay off to the side, with scribbles of a short story

I was trying to piece together. The margins marked up with poetry. On that lawn, in that July heat, I had nothing but time and my own company. I'd never felt more relaxed.

Stretched out, my fingertips hovered just above and grazed the blades of grass. And I let my hands rest on the tip-tops of the blades and gently pushed down—each blade tip pressing into my palm. Hundreds of blunt pinpricks brought everything into sharper focus. I lifted my knees and let my feet press down flat into the ground. A wash of cool breeze swept over my legs, and I let my arms fan up gently, like a snow angel in July.

No exams, no coursework. No camp, no activities. My summer jobs at the pool, the golf club, the furniture store would all come later. It was the summer of nothing noteworthy. Summer 1992, age 13-going-on-14. The last time I felt truly free.

As I revisit this memory now, it makes me really sad. Two lines in particular: "The last time I felt truly free" and "Hiding, and maintaining this facade, was exhausting." At 13, I was already living in conflict. Great marks were expected of me—from myself and my parents—and society supposedly rewarded and loved high marks. But only to a certain point, beyond which I risked the alienation of my peers. And so I became a dress-up doll of sorts, putting on the right costume for the right audience.

* * *

Now that I was starting to slow down, get some real rest, and was creating space in my calendar—it was time to fill that space with fun. The problem was: I'd completely forgotten what that was.

My friend Cara was fully on board with the big scale back and immediately insisted on a visit to her family cottage in Northern Ontario. From my perspective, this definitely seemed like something that might fall on the fun list, so I said yes without any further thought.

Barefoot, I stepped off the wooden slats of the cottage deck and on to the lightly raked earth trail that led down to the lake. As my feet pressed gently into the earth, I paused. When was the last time I'd walked with bare feet and actually felt the ground? I couldn't recall. Many, many years ago at a beach resort, perhaps. But not Canadian soil underfoot in June.

We both sat at the end of the dock, but it was my toes that dropped into the lake first. As my shins fully immersed, I lay back on the beach towel stretched out behind me and closed my eyes. As I exhaled, I felt the Ontario sun wash over my face. Just like on my terrace, as the sun touched my skin, my body softened.

How had I missed the simple joy of the sunshine for so long?

"This is what's been missing in my life," I said to Cara. My head sank into the dock slats, my jaw relaxed, and I felt the tension melt away. The delayed waves from a boat that passed minutes before lapped against the dock, rocking and lulling me into a dreamy, semi-conscious state.

"You can't go on like you have been." Cara's voice broke through the filminess enveloping me and pulled me back into the present. "You're a workaholic, Steph . . . it rendered you barely functional," she said this last part softly, tentatively, as though the words risked breaking me.

"Don't worry," I said with a smile. "I told you, I'm scaling back."

"I know, I know . . ." Her voice was laced with doubt, suggesting the opposite. "But I also know you. I worry this might just be a phase and you'll be right back to—"

"It's not a phase," I interrupted, resolute, both for her benefit and mine.

It is not a phase.

I reapplied some sunscreen, and my head fell back in full surrender.

* * *

Staring back at me from the mirror were unruly bangs and new gold hoop earrings.

One month in to the scale back and my bangs were getting long. My eyelashes twitched uncontrollably as they started to entangle with the too-long strands. I pulled them apart—one half of the bangs to one side, and the other half to the other—and pressed them into submission. A middle part. I ran my hand through the center of my scalp, pulling all the hair back and off my face. That one movement held so much freedom.

Up to that point, "polished and professional" had been the driver of my daily costume. Styling and spraying each rebellious hair strand into place. There was safety in being polished. Look the part and you were closer to being the part. Wasn't that how it worked? I'd spent years in boardrooms: the men in impeccable designer suits, socks in an array of colors—to exude a pop of creativity—anchored by tan wingtip shoes. Women in red-soled shoes, silver and gold bracelets worth thousands of dollars apiece, laptops pulled from tote bags worth many times more than most folks' monthly income.

And sure, those items can be beautiful and fun, but I had to wonder if, perhaps, we were all wearing these things in an effort to look the part. Exude status. Declare power. They were the symbols of success, signaling that you were someone to be listened to and respected. That you'd earned your place around that boardroom table. In full costume, you were somebody.

One thing I was not naturally? Polished.

And I wondered then, were any of us, really? Or were we all just wearing our polished security blankets, costumes to cover up the fear, the insecurity, and the real humanness going on inside of us all the time? Perhaps it was all one big power-playing show.

I missed jumping into pools and lakes—or sitting in a hot tub—without worrying about the proximity of a hair dryer. I was exhausted by continually battling with hair that had a life of its own—sometimes falling straight, sometimes wavy, other times a pile of partially curly frizz. I'd now spent well over a decade forcing my bangs into a fixed, submissive line across my forehead; spraying them with a concrete lacquer to hold them in place for the day.

It was absurd.

I felt myself exhale. I was done with the costume. The bangs had to go.

I wanted to live according to the whims of the woman with unpredictable hair. I wanted to be the woman who could jump in the lake at any moment, and shake her hair, wet and free, with reckless abandon.

I ran my hand through my hair again, letting it fall behind my ears and putting the new gold hoop earrings on full display. I'd spent my life longing to wear hoop earrings, but being conditioned to believe they were unprofessional or juvenile.

I wanted to live according to the whims of the woman who refused to be conditioned.

* * *

I lived in a part of Toronto known as the Beaches. It was like its own little community within the larger city, nestled right up against a beautiful stretch of Lake Ontario.

With the hot, long sunny days that are typical of Toronto summers, the Beaches came alive when the spring temperatures rose into the double digits. From sunrise to sunset, the lake was dotted with kayaks, stand-up paddle boards, jet skis, and sailboats while the white sandy beach became a second home to people of all ages. Around them, dogs, joggers, bikers, Frisbee throwers, and beach volleyball players—their bodies caked in a sweat-sand compound—took up any remaining space.

Instead of beginning my work day at 7:30 in the morning, I'd moved from my terrace mornings, and had started walking the beach every morning, settling into my work at 9 a.m.

That morning, I walked the boardwalk and took in the sounds: the click-clack of my flip-flops, which clicked and clacked at a different tempo than those of the woman a few paces in front of me; two seagulls battled over a gravy-soaked french fry mid-air; a mother ran by pushing a stroller with a sleeping toddler nestled within it; a man glided by backwards on roller skates, an old-school boom box wedged into his bicep. Next to me, a couple strolled by, their hands intertwined and their eyes alight with early-dating bliss.

In that moment, I felt freer than I had in years, possibly ever.

Two months into the scale back—bangs grown out, hoop earrings a permanent fixture, workdays beginning at 9 a.m.—and nothing had fallen apart.

No one had canceled meetings on account of my unpolishedness. No one had sent me home to fix my hair.

My work life carried on with meetings, phone calls, and deadlines. With one difference: I was feeling lighter—and happier.

This. More of this, please.

As a relatively new "Beacher," I got caught up in the beach volleyball frenzy and joined my neighbors' team that summer, having not played the game since high school gym class. And that was indoors. But the technique—the bumps, the volleys, the spikes—were all coming back to me, and I found myself looking forward to Friday nights at 6:45 when we'd meet at the net, open the coolers, sink our bare feet into the sand, and play until the sun set over the lake.

And as the sun set, and the moon rose, we flopped in the sand, and the laughter and the drinks seemed never-ending. This new freedom felt dizzying, and I laughed every Friday night, without a care in the world.

It was one of those nights at the beach that a text came in from Cara: "You're playing beach volleyball, right? Luke was up at the cottage today. His beach team needs a sub. I gave him your number."

That was the extent of the text. I'd heard of Luke for as long as I'd known Cara, which was approaching eleven years. Somehow, though, Luke and I had never met. There was always some reason or another. Our weekends at Cara's cottage never aligned, we weren't in the same social circles, and it had just never happened.

Within minutes of Cara's text, my phone lit up with a message from an unknown number: "Hey, Steph, it's Luke. Cara tells me you play beach volleyball. My team is down a girl on Tuesday night. Any chance you could sub in?"

My text back was tentative and questioning: I wasn't a great player; my league wasn't competitive; how serious were they; would they yell at me if I played badly?

He put an end to all of my questioning. "Honestly, we just need a body or else we need to forfeit," he wrote back, with a winking, smiley-faced emoji.

A body. *That* I could commit to.

Four days later, two hours out from the game, I was dressed to play and guzzling back water to hydrate when my phone rang.

It was one of my board members.

We barely exchanged hello's before he dove right in: "We need to have a call with James and Claire ASAP. They're interested in partnering."

They were our contacts at the bank, and this was potentially a big deal. "Yep, sure, I'll get something booked with them. What's your calendar like this wee—" I responded, as I pulled an open envelope off the coffee table and onto my lap and jotted a reminder to myself.

"Tonight at 6:30 works for all of us. Can you send out call details and give them some background information via email prior to the call?"

That one sentence: *it works for all of us*. As though their schedules were the only ones for consideration. As though mine was open and ready to be filled by anyone, for anything, at any time.

I gulped and planted my feet firmly on the floor, thinking: *It doesn't work for ME.*

"Tonight at 6:30?" I replied, my voice raised slightly in pitch.

"Yes." He said, in a tone that left no opening or space for alternative.

"Um, I'm afraid I can't," I heard the words coming out of my mouth. "I have plans." My tone matched his: firm, leaving no room for negotiation.

Had I just said that? Over the phone, he couldn't see my hand raising up over my mouth in surprise. For the first time in my life, I had said no to a work commitment. And for once, there was no unsaid-but-implied *but I can cancel if you need me to.*

I had a life to live on my Tuesday evening. I wasn't at everyone else's beck and call. My calendar, my schedule, was just as important as his. I had beach volleyball. That was that. This scaled back woman wasn't budging.

Stammering and fumbling on the other end of the call, he finally conceded that 4 p.m. the following day would work as well.

"Booked," I said with finality. I sent the calendar invite, penned the email to everyone involved, and closed my computer.

I'd done it. I'd stuck to my scaled back rules. And I wasn't sneaky about it. I had spoken the truth.

And nothing bad happened.

It was about a fifteen-minute walk along the boardwalk from my place to the volleyball courts, and I felt ready to skip the whole way there with glee.

I had been tested and had held firm in my boundary.

And nothing bad happened.

I flip-flopped my way across the wooden plats, taking in the early evening sun that was still warm enough for a tank top. My sweatshirt was folded over my arm for later; I assumed that we'd be in the sand late into the evening, as was the beach volleyball post-game norm.

To my right, Lake Ontario filled the space between the boardwalk and the horizon. To my left, the bike trail ran adjacent to the board-walk. On the boardwalk, I maneuvered around children, dogs, couples, and groups of teenagers poking and play-fighting with each other.

The neighborhood was alive. All around me were women who were clearly not thinking about work. They were laughing, joyful and enjoying an evening on the beach. Dotted along the sand were blankets and picnic baskets, Frisbees and footballs. Here was this workaholic-free zone right in my backyard. What had I been missing for all these years?

I'm here now.

And I slowed my pace.

As I approached the volleyball courts, I could hear the beat of the music as it pumped out across the vast expanse of courts, as players gathered to begin their warm ups. I glanced at my phone, and Luke's text: Court 56.

It was odd: usually, new people and a competitive sport game would have me nervous. But tonight, as I walked up to court 56, to join a bunch of strangers, to play a game I'd only reconnected to a few weeks ago, I felt nothing but excitement. Maybe it was the sun beating down, or maybe it was saying no to the board member only hours ago, but as I approached a tall, tanned, broad-shouldered, curly-haired, tank top wearing guy and called out "Luke?" I just knew that this—right here—was exactly where I was meant to be.

Luke's face broke into a wide grin. "Steph? You made it!" He tossed the volleyball to me. "Show us what you got!"

We won the game.

Tori, the other woman on the team, couldn't stay, and so it was me, Luke, and Jay, the other guy, who sunk into the sand after the game. Luke's arm reached into the cooler and he passed me an apple cider. "Nice work tonight, champ," he joked as I took the can from his hand. Our eyes locked.

For the last couple of hours, I'd been laser focused on the actual game, not wanting to let the team down. But now, I was laser focused on what was right in front of me: Luke, Jay, and the apple cider.

The three of us talked about anything and everything. Mostly nonsense with lots of laughter. Jay's mini stereo pumped out tune after tune, and Luke kept the stories coming. The cooler had a seemingly endless supply, and the evening hours of Tuesday night stretched out for hours, one joke at a time.

When we finally packed up for the night, Luke turned to me, his mouth set in a half-smile. "Let me drive you home," he said more as a statement than a question. We both knew I was well within walking distance.

As he dropped me off, he quipped, "Hey, we may need you there again sometime."

I stepped out of his truck and peeked my head back inside smiling. "I don't doubt it." And with that, I shut the door and headed to my front door.

As I settled in to bed that night, I thought of Luke, and of the sand, the ciders, the laughter.

More of this, too, please. Much more of this.

* * *

Turns out, there was much more of that to come. I became a cheerleading fixture at the Tuesday night games. And Luke and me? Well, we've been together ever since those volleyball games so many years ago.

UNHOOKING FROM PERSONALITY CONSTRAINTS

As the scale back continued, the fantasies of resigning visited me often, though I knew that I couldn't resign from my role overnight. First of all, I had a responsibility to transition out of the role properly (if leaving was the decision that eventually felt right to me); and second of all, I had financial obligations that made resigning quickly nonnegotiable.

When I explored different possibilities, I uncovered an interesting option: Could I turn this frenetic, demanding, over-committed role into one that allowed for balance, ease, and a feeling of peace? In other words: Was the frenetic, demanding, over-commitment just the nature of a big role? Or was it me and my Enneagram Type 9 *self-forgetting* behaviors—like a lack of boundaries and a fear of "shutting off and unplugging" in case I disappointed someone—that were getting in my way? Could I redefine the way I got work done?

I was both excited and terrified. And of course, because I was contemplating big change, all kinds of fear and resistance showed up, as well as my limiting beliefs. I was also coming up against the society-approved unconscious productivity loop. I was secretly convinced that there were only two options: suck it up, put on the corporate mask, and suffer through the corporate world pretending to be an aggressive, ladder-climbing hyper-productive executive *or* quit my job and face financial ruin. Other phrases that looped through my mind at this time:

So, what am I going to do? Quit my job and go bankrupt?

You should be thankful for this job.

You just need to toughen up—others get by just fine working these hours.

This is what it means to be successful.

You owe it to your parents for all the money they spent on your education.

No pain, no gain.

So you want to just slack off and be lazy?

Any of these sound familiar?

Doubt and fear can create all kinds of narratives. When this happens, revisit the *new beliefs* you identified in Chapter 6. As a reminder, mine were:

Joy, rest, and socializing don't need to be earned.

I am more than my work.

My definition of success includes my health and happiness.

When I would reread that list, I would ask myself: *Is this unreasonable?* And the answer, of course, was no. Revisiting these statements whenever I felt fear or doubt helped to anchor me into these new beliefs.

My fears and doubts at this time were simply the desperate pleas of limiting beliefs and personality constraints trying to stay relevant.

When you are in the midst of change, remind yourself of this, and often: ***your fears and doubts are almost always your limiting beliefs and personality constraints making a desperate attempt to stay relevant.***

One of the toughest changes, for me, was (and still is) unhooking from my Enneagram Type 9 personality constraint of *self-forgetting*. I had never set boundaries with anyone in my life and yet, boundary-setting was now a critical skill if I was going to live into my new beliefs and create the life I desired for myself. Think about the role your Enneagram personality patterns play in your new belief system. What do you, specifically, need to unhook from? What skill will help you to unhook?

Turns out, undoing well over a decade of work habits wasn't easy.

My biggest obstacle to my new boundaried, scaled back lifestyle was my smartphone. This is now widely discussed. A 2016 survey from Deloitte found that Americans collectively check their phones eight billion times per day. We know about prominent tech executives who are now coming forward to speak of the addictive and neurological issues with our devices, most notably Tristan Harris, former design ethicist at Google, who is now the president and cofounder of the Center for Humane Technology.

But back when I was declaring the scale back, these discussions weren't as prevalent—at least not in my world. In my professional circles, our smartphones were a fixture in our lives that lured us in and kept us working all hours of the day and night. As I started to slow down and really pay attention to what my inner knowing was trying to tell me, I noticed that my device was a big part of the problem. I could literally *feel* my nervous system shift into high alert as soon as my phone vibrated or dinged. My shoulders would tense and my heart rate would rise as my thumbs moved rapidly across the screen.

My phone was triggering my stress response. At all hours of the day, every day.

And so setting firm boundaries with my device was the first step: no looking at the phone before 8 a.m. or after 7 p.m. No looking at emails on Saturdays or on Sundays before 8 p.m.

This felt like a massive rebellion, but it was immediately restorative and transformational.

One of my favorite experts on habit formation is James Clear (author of *Atomic Habits*). He speaks about the work of creating new habits, and one of the critical steps is forming a new identity. In my case, I was looking to shift my identity from the *self-forgetting, work-before-all-else, productivity addict* I was when under the spell of unconscious productivity to a *boundaried, balanced, responsible* leader of my own life, firmly anchored in conscious productivity.

According to Clear, once you are clear on the identity shift you are looking to make, you then determine the actions and habits that someone with that identity embodies.

In my case, a *boundaried, balanced, responsible* leader looked like:

- Someone who respects their own boundaries checks their email periodically and intentionally.

- Someone who respects their own boundaries has a morning routine that doesn't include screen time.
- Someone who is responsible balances personal and professional responsibilities.
- Someone who is balanced identifies what is essential in all areas of their life.

And so on. Each time I stuck to these habits, I was collecting evidence and reinforcement that, yes, I *could* be and, in fact, was becoming, a *boundaried, balanced, responsible* leader of my own life, firmly anchored in conscious productivity.

This approach to habit formation is critical, because when you first start out, you may not trust yourself. And you are doing the work of changing your identity. So having a clear idea of the actions and habits that align with "someone who is that particular identity" and then enacting those actions and habits yourself, helps you to start to trust yourself with this new identity, providing you with evidence and reinforcement that, yes, you *are* becoming that new identity. Habit by habit, action by action.

And talk about *conscious*. Once I started identifying the actions and habits of the person I wanted to be (that is, the person I knew I *was* underneath all of that past conditioning), putting them into practice (and noticing how much better I felt as a result), I couldn't now *unknow* this new approach. Every time I violated one of these new habits or slipped into old habits, I was very aware of it. I was able to catch myself in the moment and course correct.

CLARITY: WHAT DO YOU KNOW **FOR SURE**

At this point in the process—when things can still feel confusing or half-baked—I want you to think about *what you know for sure* at this point. This is a list of learnings that you would like to lock in. Personal examples from my "what I know for sure" list:

- I know I love corporate coaching.
- I know I'm fascinated by leadership and interpersonal dynamics in the workplace.
- I know I am more fulfilled and creative when I unplug for twenty-four hours straight at some point in the week.
- I know that time in nature restores me.
- I know that I come up with some of my best ideas when I'm *not* sitting at my desk.
- I know I want to work with, and for, people who value self-aware-ness and growth.
- I know I want to work in a way that allows space for more bal-ance across all areas of my life.
- I know that I move through my day with more ease and grace when I start my day journaling and away from screens.

During the scale back, I had no idea how I was going to bring all of these puzzle pieces together, but I knew for sure that, for me, these statements were absolute truths.

In addition to what you know for sure, I want you to think about *how you want to feel*. I first learned of this concept when reading

Danielle LaPorte's *Desire Map*. In this book, she challenges readers to rethink how they approach goal setting in their lives. Instead of thinking about goals as a list of tasks, she suggests starting with *how you want to feel in your life*. And then identify goals that bring you closer to those feelings.

I find this to be especially helpful when I'm not sure about the specifics of my future vision. I may not know what it looks like, but I can *imagine how I want to feel*. For example, in the personal stories I've shared with you so far, you may have noticed a common theme: I wanted to feel more autonomy, more freedom, and I certainly wanted more space in my life for non-work-related activities. My "Core Desired Feelings" (as LaPorte would call them) at that time included: freedom, autonomy, spaciousness, and connection. And remember, I didn't yet know *how* I was going to create this freedom, but I knew it was how I wanted to feel.

Starting with how you want to feel puts you in direct contact with your inner knowing. Rather than looking outside yourself to what *others* are doing and achieving, you go inward to determine how you want to feel in your life. Once you've determined how you want to *feel and be* in your life, you have a lens through which to assess what you want to *do* in your life, and *how* you want to do it.

If you want to feel *secure* in your life, you might design your life very differently than someone who wants to feel *innovative*.

Two executive leaders—one who wants to feel *generous* and one who wants to feel *important*—will likely thrive in different environments.

A parent who wants to feel *connected* might make different parenting choices than one who wants to feel *inspirational*.

This is why conscious productivity—and tuning into your own inner knowing—is so transformational. Instead of comparing ourselves to others who might be in the same role of parent, or leader, and questioning ourselves against *them and how they do it*, we hold ourselves up to our own definition of how we want to feel and be in the world.

I want you to think about the feelings that you are looking to bring into your life. To help you with this, you may want to have a list of feeling words handy (feelingswheel.com is a great resource, or consult a thesaurus or dictionary). Try to get as specific as possible. Give yourself the chance to land on the feeling words that feel *just right*. These feelings will now offer you clues and guidance about how to design your life, deliberately, and on purpose.

COMMITMENT: WHAT DO YOU **KNOW** YOU WANT TO CHANGE

Go back over your notes and responses from the last chapter: consider the new beliefs you want to create, what you are desiring for your life, and what you want to change. Go digging for gold! Remind yourself about what your current state is costing you, what you know for sure, and how you want to feel.

Taking in that information, what are you ready to commit to? You may be tempted to list numerous commitments, but trying to commit to twenty different changes in your life might be challenging and may not be the best way to set yourself up for success. Brainstorm and jot down as many commitments as you can think of, then pare down the list (keep all of your ideas for future reference, though). I want you to start by landing on *one thing*, one behavior, pattern, belief, or feeling you'd like to unpack and work with first. You can come back to the others later.

Think about which one is going to give you traction right away and help you to move toward the feelings you've identified and the things you know for sure. Think about the connection between the commitment you're making and the specific limiting belief or personality constraint you're looking to break, the feelings you want to feel, and what you know for sure. By making this connection clear for yourself, you'll be able to remind yourself of this connection when the change feels challenging or hard (which it inevitably will at some point).

CURATION: COLLECT YOUR GIFTS AND TALENTS

We spent a lot of time talking about the things that you *don't want* or *don't like* and limiting beliefs and personality constraints that *aren't serving you*. Now I want you to reflect on all of your strengths, gifts, and talents. Here, I want you to list *everything* that is a talent or gift of yours—anything from being able to choose the perfect paint color for a space through to mediating conflict and disagreement in the workplace. This is also a good time to review your personality patterns (*refer to the Enneagram chart on page 63*).

I often joke with my clients: "There are oh so many things that you *aren't* gifted at, so I want you to really and truly claim those things you *are* gifted at!" By thinking of it through this lens, it may help you to feel more comfortable owning what you're really good at (especially if you were raised to value humility). For myself, I know that my musical talent is *very* limited. Sure, I could invest in lessons and make myself *better*, but musical ability is not a natural gift or talent of mine. But active listening and relating to people sure is. Knowing that there are many areas of life where I'm exceptionally below average (cooking is another example, as is navigational ability), actually frees me up to celebrate those areas where I am *above average and excellent*. I want you to do this exercise for yourself.

Think back over your life—going back to childhood—and identify things that are natural talents and gifts of yours. Pick things that you can really claim and really believe in.

Next, I want you to think about the things that you've experienced in your work life and career that, when you're being really honest with yourself, you're not that good at, and then create two separate lists: (1) "Things I'm not that good at . . . yet." This list may include things that you want to invest in, to build and develop your strength and ability in that area; (2) "Things I'm not that good at . . . and ideally, I never want to do this again." For this list, I want you to itemize exactly that: the duties, responsibilities, tasks that you, ideally, would never want to do again in your professional life.

The final list I want you to create—and where things can get *very* interesting—is a list of things that you're good at, perhaps even *known for,* that—truth be told—you don't enjoy doing. Why is this so interesting? Because this is often when we can get stuck in our careers and end up feeling unfulfilled.

Perhaps you climbed the corporate ladder, only to discover you actually don't enjoy managing people—and miss being an individual contributor.

Maybe you've been highly praised for your speaking abilities, but you feel completely drained whenever you have to present to a group.

Maybe you're the top seller at your company, yet you can't stand the industry or product you're selling.

I remember the moment I realized that—if I was being completely honest—I didn't enjoy operational oversight. And yet I'd often been praised and promoted specifically because of this skill. But . . . I loved leadership and knew that operational oversight was typically a critical leadership responsibility. When I wrote those words down on paper, it felt terrifying. And it also felt like the absolute truth.

When we're good at something—are praised for it, promoted for it, valued for it, and celebrated for it—it can be really tempting to stay in that role, on that career path, even though it's something that you know—on a soul level—you don't enjoy doing. For this list, you may write down entire industries or roles or tasks within roles. Key here is to be honest with yourself. You don't need to share this list with anyone yet, nor do you need to make any decisions. Just make the unconscious, conscious.

Now that you've started really gathering the clues, and some critical information about yourself and what you want and don't want, use this information to guide you, and continue to move in the direction of what *fulfills* you. Notice that, at this point, you still may not have articulated specifically what your ideal future goal or state is. That's okay.

Notice how this process is helping you to gather more information and to be a detective in your own life by gathering clues. And once you've gathered these clues, you can use this information to continue to guide you to move in the direction of fulfillment. You're continuing to gather information that can help you continue to take action—even if it's *imperfect action*. This is a process of *ongoing refinement*. As you continue this process of ongoing refinement, you're going to get closer and closer to fulfillment—you'll have pockets and moments of fulfillment on the journey—as you determine your ultimate destination.

WORKSHEET

CLARITY, COMMITMENT, AND CURATION

Commitment: What are you ready to commit to changing in your life?

Clarity: What do you know for sure?

Curation: Think back over your career and complete the following four columns:

Things I'm good at that I love . . .
Things I'm not good at, yet . . .
Things I'm not good at (and don't care to be) . . .
Things I'm good at, but don't enjoy doing . . .

CHAPTER 8

HONORING YOUR CONSTITUTION AND WHO YOU ARE

Dating life with Luke was pure fun, so it didn't surprise me when he suggested a weekend away. He asked if I wanted to go to Cara's cottage for a three-day getaway, just the two of us. "I mean, it would be great research for the scale back," he said with a smile.

I heard myself saying, without pause, "I'm in."

And so there I was, standing in the kitchen, waiting for him to pick me up and whisk me away for an idyllic Northern Ontario getaway.

He arrived to pick me up and our plan had been to pick up groceries together somewhere on the way. Instead, as I began loading my weekend bag in the back of the truck, I noticed grocery bags overflowing in the backseat. Well, truth be told, it was his arms I noticed first, as they reached for my overnight bag and placed it in among the weekend supplies. Those arms carried their fair share of his six foot two, 250-pound broad frame.

He smiled a smile of sheepishness, pride, and excitement. "So . . . I did a little shopping," he said. He'd filled the truck with food—curated from stores across the city. Packaged and chilled were thick-cut steaks, cheeses, root vegetables diced and marinating in giant Ziploc bags, and everything required for the greasiest of breakfast sandwiches.

Who was this man?!

I wanted to beam us to the cottage, for the rest of the world to fade into the background, and leave the two of us alone, with nothing but steaks, a fire, and a blanket.

As though reading my mind, he reached over to take the bag from my other hand. "Okay, let's get to this cottage already. My plan is for us to be on the dock with drinks in hand by four o'clock, followed by dinner cooked entirely by campfire."

"I like everything about that plan," I said as we pulled away from my building.

At 3:58 p.m., our canoe pulled up to the dock of Cara's boat-access-only cottage. We jumped from the canoe, pulled out the cooler, and popped open some drinks. Our feet crossed out in front of us, drinks in hand, the canoe tied to the dock with the steaks bobbing with the waves, we leaned back on our elbows and let the late afternoon sun wash over us. Hands grazing, our cans chinked as we uttered a "cheers" and marked the kickoff to our weekend.

Within an hour, the sun that we'd been soaking up was well hidden behind thick black clouds, and the rain began pelting the cottage. Looking out the far window at the firepit—now being pummeled with rain—I giggled. "Ahh, the best-laid plans. So much for dinner by campfire!" I said.

Luke's eyes flashed with the mischievous determination of a man ready for any challenge. "For every problem, there is a solution." Without another word, I watched from the kitchen window as he made his way down to the lakeside, and soaked, he dismantled the umbrella that was bolted to the dock, brought it back to the firepit, and fashioned us our own little bistro. Under the striped canopy of the umbrella was a roaring campfire and bench space for two, complete with cooking utensils and cups for wine. He came back into the cottage, his shirt clinging to him with rainwater, firepit tongs in hand, and said, "What did I tell you?" He pointed at the campfire with the tongs. "Problem? Solution. Now pass me those steaks, please."

I handed him the steaks without saying a word, because everything about the last fifteen minutes had left me speechless.

As he walked back out to the fire, cutting board loaded down with meat, I had a moment of disbelief that the two of us were here, at Cara's cottage. I thought about all the weekends I'd spent, alone and working—always working—for well over a decade. I realized, then, that I hadn't had a single thought about work since he'd picked me up. I hadn't checked my phone or computer for messages.

I felt alive—and *happy*. This, I realized, was what my productivity addiction had been costing me all these years. Hustling for my worth had robbed me of these simple but magical moments.

We sat under that umbrella next to that campfire for hours, talking about things serious and ridiculous in between bites of steak, all of it intensified by the wall of rain coming down all around us. He told me about his family's farm and his desire to get out of the city as often as possible. I talked about the scale back and how my new way of working was completely at odds with everything I'd been taught about the corporate world.

We talked about the ridiculousness of bureaucracy, over administration, and meetings for the sake of meetings; about greed, and overidentification with roles and money. We talked about our mutual love of *Arrested Development*, about ambition, and finally about hustle culture, which I sheepishly admitted, I was in the midst of untangling from but was still very much enmeshed with.

"There's always talk of Type A's," I said. We'd moved inside and were curled up on the futon of the screened-in porch, my head resting on his shoulder and one leg draped over his knee. "But I've never heard anyone talk about Type B's. I think people might assume that being a Type B means being lazy, but I don't think that's it at all," I said, my free hand twisting a section of my hair around and around. "The Type A's may always be buzzing about, looking busy, but it doesn't mean they get more done—or get it done well. I think I'm an aspiring Type B—whatever that might be—and I think a Type B can get just as much done and have a hell of a lot more fun along the way . . ." I let my voice trail off, and my eyes close, feeling only the strength of his shoulder holding my head up.

I felt his head nodding above mine. "It's all about choosing what to care about, and almost more importantly, *not* care about," he said.

I looked up at him, watching him search his mind for the right next words, and his smile broadened as he continued. "You know, like selective caring." I realized then that Luke epitomized the Type B personality.

Selective caring. I repeated it back to myself. *Yes.*

I let the words sink in. "Selective caring," I said out loud this time, and turned to him with a smile. "I think you're onto something there."

* * *

The summer of the scale back continued, and I sunk into new feelings of rest, joy, and fun. It felt SO good to have a life. Seriously. As I moved through weekends and life with Luke, I experienced a freedom, a joy, and a connection with life and love I'd never experienced before. I went full days without considering work, without checking my phone. We had so much *fun.* What I noticed over time is that he held no fixed beliefs about ambition, about *how work was supposed to be.* He couldn't have cared less about corporate ladders.

He wasn't attracted to me because of my work success and prospects. He also wasn't threatened or repelled because of my work success and prospects. He held zero attachment to my success.

What he *did* hold, though, was support for my goals and dreams. He listened attentively about my dream of writing a book and starting my own business.

And I thought: *THIS is what support looks and feels like.*

I also noticed how he moved through the world—he was always

completely present. If he was having a conversation, he was all in. He was never distracted, never checking his phone, his mind was never wandering. If he was working on a building project, he was focused on that project, giving it his full attention. When his body felt tired, he napped. He took breaks, had a beer or two. And then he'd resume what needed to get done. He'd sit up late at the campfire, joking and socializing one weekend, and the next, he may be in bed at 9 p.m. No apologies, no explanation, other than: "I'm really tired today."

Luke was a special force. He seemed to be part unknowing Yoda, part earth element, and part just awesome, funny, smart guy. What I knew was when I was around him, something shifted. Time slowed down, I felt calm, and I felt present. These were states I hadn't felt— either collectively or individually—well, *ever*.

Here's what I noticed about Luke. He had a full-time job, he was a part-time parent, and he also did significant contracting work for colleagues and neighbors. Yet he was never stressed.

He honored his responsibilities; he never missed deadlines, he took on passion projects, and he had a heck of a lot of fun. He checked in with himself about what he wanted and what he needed, while being mindful of the responsibilities he needed to manage. And joy and fun were *always* part of his criteria, which was a completely novel concept to me.

More of this, please.

I realized I'd become fixed in an either/or dichotomy of "I can either be responsible OR I can have fun and joy." I hadn't been act-ively thinking this, of course—it was an unconscious belief I'd held, well, unconsciously. Luke made this belief of mine conscious—and experiencing him and how he lived his life beautifully challenged this long-held unconscious belief.

Now that it was conscious, I couldn't unlearn it. I didn't want to. What would be possible for me in a life where I both honored my responsibilities *and* had joy and fun?

* * *

I felt like I had it all. I was finding a balance between my work and personal life; I was hitting my targets at work; I had a fabulous relationship with Luke; and I had more time for my friends and family. And my health issues? The insomnia, headaches, stress, and adrenal issues all melted away.

Wouldn't it be great if the story ended there? I uncovered the hidden beliefs that were holding me back, met Luke, and lived my life of joy, fun, and appropriate responsibility without any further disruption to my life?

That wasn't my experience, and I'll be honest, it's not the experience of my clients once they start uncovering real, deep truths and beliefs that they've been ruled by for their entire lives. There may be a short period of glee and feelings of freedom after the initial realization: "This! THIS is what's been holding me back for all these years! I'm free!"

But shortly after this realization comes another one: Wait—I've built my entire life around these beliefs—my career, my relationships, my finances.

As I started putting work boundaries in place—and as people started to notice that it wasn't a passing phase or just recovery from an illness, but an actual change I was making—the challenges began. I had people trying to regain control over my schedule, imposing impossible deadlines, serving up guilt trips.

And I couldn't really blame them. They'd hired a pleaser. I was changing the game on them; I was showing up differently. They'd hired someone who placed work ahead of literally everything else—including her health. My organizations always won. Always. Yes, I was smart and talented, but so are many people. What *really* had given me an edge was that I sacrificed *everything else* for my companies. Why wouldn't bosses, board members, and stakeholders love that? Why would they discourage that? I'd set a bar of work that required me to have zero personal life, zero boundaries, and no identity other than work.

Once I embarked on the scale back, there was no going back for me. Once I'd had a glimpse, a taste, of joy and happiness—or what could exist in those hours outside of head-down productivity—I knew I was on the right path. But it wasn't an easy path. Every aspect of my life and my way of perceiving and reacting to the world had to change.

And with it, my friendships and close relationships changed. My job changed. My beliefs changed. Until I got right down to the core, to my essence. All these masks of identity—roles I played, roles I was given—needed to be removed.

Who was I at my essence?

Would I find out?

These were the thoughts tumbling through my mind when I got in the thick of the scale back. But I knew a few things for sure. When living under the constraints of my limiting beliefs and personality:

I was miserable.

I felt alone.

I had a very strong sense that I was "off track."

I was exhausted.

And I had a very strong sense that there was a better way for me to be living. That it was possible to feel more *aligned.* That I was here to do *something,* and that *something* was not how I had been approaching my life for so long.

I needed to fundamentally shift.

And learn to trust my voice over others. I was—and still am—so good at reading others, sensing what they want and need and feel that I sometimes end up taking on their wants, needs, and feelings as my own and have trouble separating *me* from *them.* And because of that, I was constantly:

. . . second-guessing myself

. . . overriding my own knowing

. . . pleasing and appeasing others

. . . not rocking the boat

. . . stepping back, and operating from the background.

I had to change *all* of that.

It felt uncomfortable and scary at many points along the journey—but what kept me committed was that feeling of ease, joy, and balance. I finally knew that those feelings were possible for me—and I wasn't willing to let them go. That provided some powerful stick-with-it-ness, even when times got tough.

HONORING YOUR CONSTITUTION

In the last chapter we talked about clarity, commitment, and curation. I asked you to identify how you want to *feel* in your ideal future state and to take an inventory of your gifts and talents, as well as those things that you're good at (but don't actually like to do) and those things that (if you're honest) you'd never like to do again.

This was very focused on *doing* and *action*. Now I want to focus more on the *being* and "*how*" aspects of yourself. Or what I consider your unique constitution. The literal definition of *constitution* is *the physical makeup of the body, including its functions, metabolic processes, and reactions to stimuli.* The way I think of constitution is being in alignment with your body's rhythms and optimal conditions. **Your constitution has less to say about *what* you do and more about *how* you do it.** Understanding your constitution and honoring it is a critical factor in feeling fulfilled and content.

We humans are not machines. We are not designed to operate at full capacity all the time. And yet the world of unconscious productivity drives us to work that way, and rewards us for it. Our bodies are wise, and if we don't honor our rhythms, the body will correct for it (hence why I found myself repeatedly suffering from adrenal crashes).

When I found myself frustrated and resentful in corporate life when my calendar would be booked—not only back-to-back, but double and sometimes *triple* booked for the same time slots—I knew something had to change. With the calendar so rammed, I was less present, less creative, and it meant strategic work that required deeper thought had to be pushed to the evening. *This is no way to work,* I'd mutter to myself.

And the research backs this: ideally for focus, creativity, and optimal energy management, we humans are best suited to match our ultradian rhythms, which in simple terms, is our body's basic rest–activity cycle. When we're awake, we move from higher to lower alertness every ninety minutes. Once I started paying attention to this rhythm, I could sense these ebbs and flows, and changed my work habits accordingly. As I started to pay more attention to my own constitution, the more I learned my body's wisdom—it was always signaling to me about what I needed, and my optimal conditions. Once I stopped overriding that wisdom with my limiting belief of "work comes first—*always*—power through," not only did I feel better, but I generated better quality outcomes, faster. What wisdom is your body—your constitution—trying to share with you about the way you work best?

This is the part in the process where you really need to be rooted in a desire to change—*and* to anchor into all the work you've done so far. Because this is the part in the process where you *may* start to rock the boat or challenge what others have come to think of you. When it comes to our constitution and our optimal conditions, judgment can come into play. Both self-judgment and the judgment of others.

Our limiting beliefs, and our personality constraints, have very strong opinions about what we should and shouldn't do—you know all about that from the work in Chapter 1. Our constitutions are not immune from this judgment. Your limiting beliefs may cause you to be very harsh with yourself and your body's rhythms ("Why am I so weak?"; "Why can't I get by on five hours sleep?"). Or you may be judged by others, based on their limiting beliefs ("Why can't *they* get by on five hours sleep? Don't they know we need to power through?").

This is why this process requires courage and anchoring yourself to your new beliefs (and what your former beliefs were costing you)— because the journey will get rocky at times. When I started unplugging on weeknights, and for the bulk of the weekend, I was going against some very established industry norms—and directly against the habits and behaviors of my colleagues.

When I started giving myself breaks throughout the day—thirty minutes at a time!—I was going against the typical business practices of back-to-back meetings. When I started prioritizing a good night's sleep over getting ahead on tomorrow's tasks, I was going against my own career-long habit.

But I was honoring my constitution, and it felt great. My body— mentally, physically, emotionally, and spiritually—was at its best that summer of the scale back. But others took a great deal of offence, some of whom were outraged, at what I was doing.

Your current relationship dynamics—be it with your family, your spouse, your children, your boss, your colleagues, your direct reports, your friends and neighbors—they are used to you showing up as you always have done. And now, all of a sudden, you will be showing up differently. Behaving differently. Reacting differently. This may have an impact on them; and they may not like it. Your boss may not like the idea of you unplugging more often on the weekend. Your friends may not understand why you aren't staying out late on certain nights of the week in favor of better sleep.

But *you* will know that these changes are serving your new beliefs and honoring what your body needs.

You may never have given your constitution much thought. At the end of this chapter, you'll find a worksheet that will support you in uncovering more information about yourself, your body's optimal conditions, and other preferences. By doing this work, you'll get *conscious* about how you work best and under what conditions. Remember, with conscious productivity, you are still *producing* and *doing*—you are just getting conscious and clear about *what you're doing* and *how you're doing it*. You are the leader and designer of your own life and are creating success by your own definition.

Who do you want to be?

Underpinning my big scale back was trying on a new persona: what might it feel like to be a *boundaried, balanced, responsible* leader of my own life? For me, it felt joyful and exhilarating. Those positive feelings helped in two ways: (1) they kept me committed to my new beliefs (it felt so good to feel good!) and (2) they made me curious: how could I bring *more* of this into my life, and make it a permanent way of living?

When embarking on personal development work, one critical "stick-with-it-ness" tip is to consciously connect to what your desired state—your new belief structure—is *offering you*. We talked earlier about what your current state is *costing* you. And that is a great place to start and build momentum to drive the process. But to maintain and sustain it, look to what your desired future *offers to you*.

Understanding how the changes you are making connect to your bigger picture—the life you want to be living, the person you want to be—is critical. Sure, cottage docks and ciders with Luke were fantastic and felt great, but it wasn't *really* about the cottage or the ciders. It was about honoring my body's rhythms, giving myself a chance to rest, and creating balance across all areas of my life. **I wanted to be someone who balanced and enjoyed purposeful work *and* a loving relationship *and* a creative life. That was my new definition of success.**

So when people started to say, "Why are you spending so much time at the cottage?" or "You never come out anymore" or "I couldn't reach you on the weekend," it didn't land as criticism to me. While I had to navigate these questions and contemplate my responses (and sometimes feelings were hurt), they were part of the behavior change that was allowing me to live into my new belief system, honor my constitution, and unhook from my personality constraint of *self-forgetting*.

Now, I'd like you to think about your own bigger picture—the bigger vision you hold for yourself and your life. If you live into your new belief structure, who will you become? What is possible for you? How will you feel?

Remember unconscious productivity and its society-generated ideals of what "success" and "ambition" mean—always striving, always wanting more. Some of the most powerful and inspiring changes I've seen in clients is when their bigger vision for themselves and their lives involves doing *less*, not *more*. Getting laser focused on a few key things in their lives (and fully committing to those fewer, more meaningful things) or choosing to live more simply. Their bigger vision includes shedding commitments, relationships, and other aspects of life that no longer serve them.

Conscious productivity is about tuning in to your inner wisdom to create your *optimal-quality life*. Beware the conditioning that "more" is always better. Sometimes *spacious* and *less* provides greater riches, literally and metaphorically.

Reminder: For when the going gets tough

Making changes in life can be hard. Here are some reminders for when the going gets tough (and know that the tough part won't last forever). If you'd like a printable version, visit the *Resources* section at stephaniewoodward.com.

- **Be ready for others to be upset and push back.** While you are feeling better than you've ever felt—and feel like you are really on to something with your new approach to life and new habits—any time you change your behavior, it creates change and disruption for others in your life. They may be very comfortable, satisfied, and served by you remaining exactly as you've always been. Bottom line: don't expect others to celebrate with you as you're making changes. It doesn't necessarily mean you're doing anything wrong. It might just mean that you are creating discomfort and disruption for *them*. That said, I'm a big proponent of having open and honest conversations with the important people in your life when you are making changes (so that it doesn't catch them by surprise).

- **Be ready to provide context.** You don't need to feel obligated to provide *all* the details or to justify or rationalize yourself, nor do you owe explanations to strangers or people that aren't in your inner circle. But for those you care about and respect, it can be helpful to provide them with some context about why you are embarking on some life changes, and if appropriate, engage them in the process or be specific about the support you'd like from them.

- **It doesn't always end nicely or comfortably.** Not everyone will be happy with your decisions and changes. When you take a stand or set a boundary, you sometimes crash up against someone else's limiting belief or personality constraint. This might have them react defensively or angrily. Remember when I took a vacation and that executive threatened to drown me? Turns out, he had been without a vacation for many, many years. By taking a stand for my vacation time, I crashed right into a sensitive spot of his. Depending on the sphere of life in which you are making the changes, you may get a number of reactions.

- **It isn't easy.** Going up against the limiting beliefs and patterns that you've lived with your entire life is no simple feat! You'll slip up, get frustrated, fall back into old patterns, piss some people off, and feel very uncomfortable while you're disentangling yourself. But is it worth it? I certainly think so. You just need to wade through some muckiness to get to the other side.

WORKSHEET

BECOME AN EXPERT IN YOU

Spend some time thinking about your constitution, your body's natural rhythms, and your optimal conditions.

- What are your ideal sleeping habits? (e.g., how many hours of sleep are ideal for you? Ideal bed time? Ideal wake time?)

- When does your energy peak and wane throughout the day?

- Are there times of day when you are best suited to doing certain tasks or certain types of work?

- In what conditions do you thrive?

WORKSHEET

- How do you replenish your energy when you feel depleted?

- How would you describe your ideal work day?

- How would you describe your best non-work day?

- What lights you up? (or: what gives you energy?)

- What drains you? (or: what saps your energy?)

- What do you want more of in your life?

- What do you want less of in your life?

CHAPTER 9

YOUR WHOLE LIFE VISION

As I rested and recovered and spent more time with Luke, I felt like a new person and had new vigor and energy for my work. Turns out, taking proper time for fun, relaxation, and restoration allowed me to show up better for my other responsibilities.

I was walking between meetings when I spotted two of my former colleagues coming toward me.

"Jen! Michelle!" I exclaimed as our paths literally crossed right there at the stoplights at King Street and University Avenue in Toronto. I'd always loved working with the two of them, and with my new commitment to taking lunch breaks and *fun*, I suggested that we run into each other—deliberately and on purpose—for lunch the following week.

And so, one week later, we found ourselves sitting together, just like old times, at an overly priced restaurant in the financial district, sipping drinks and eating Nicoise salads with a bread basket wedged in between our plates.

"I barely recognize you, you're so tanned!" Jen exclaimed. "Even though it's been years and years, we all miss you back at the office. How's the new gig going?"

The word "gig" had me cringing. Oh how I wish it were just a gig. Gig made it sound so light and playful, two words that had not described my work experience for the last while. Instead of putting on the corporate polished costume and issuing enthusiastic things-couldn't-be-better proclamations with a big smile on my face, I decided to share a version of the truth. "It's been an intense year. I'm actually trying out a new approach right now . . . I'm, um, scaling back," I said, and paused as I took in their blank expressions. "It basically means less work time, more replenishing time," I said, and then pointed at my tanned arms in an effort to lighten the conversation. "Hence the tan."

Jen placed her drink back on the table and reached her hand across the bread basket and squeezed my elbow. Her eyes narrowed. "So . . . what? You're looking for another job? I may have some leads for you."

I smiled to myself. Of course that would be the assumption. "Uh, nope," I replied, shaking my head slowly and meeting her gaze. "Not at all. Quite the opposite."

She looked perplexed, and I could almost feel her mind churning, searching for the next comment or question. "So . . . you're just not working hard?"

"It's more that I'm prioritizing what's essential. Honestly, I could work twenty-four hours a day, seven days a week, and there would still be more to do. And there are plenty of people who'd love me to work that hard. Who would admire me for working that hard." I smiled, then took a big bite of crispy buttered baguette.

Michelle's expression suggested I was speaking a foreign language, while Jen's face scrunched into a scowl.

I continued once I'd swallowed the baguette deliciousness. "I just don't want to do that. Work like that. There's got to be a better way. You know?" I searched their faces for understanding but was met with blank stares. I decided to try another angle. "I mean, I got really sick." Still, nothing. They just sat there and waited for me to say more.

I didn't know what to say next. How could I best explain the why and how of the scale back; to articulate this transformation I was feeling in my mindset, my outlook, and my overall well-being?

Jen was the one to break the silence, her brow still furrowed, "But . . . aren't you worried about getting fired?" she said softly, her eyes wide.

I was getting frustrated. "I'm still managing the business and working," I tried again to explain. "I'm just not working all the time. I'm just—"

"Yeah, scaling back. We heard you," Michelle cut in, her voice like that of a mother issuing a warning to a misbehaving child. "Well, I think you're crazy. You're going to get fired. Or at the very least, this scaled back lifestyle of yours won't last past the summer." As she looked up from her food and met my gaze, her face softened slightly, and she added with a slight giggle, "You're fucking nuts. But you certainly have a great tan. You look great. I'll give you that."

With that, she took a big gulp of the drink in front of her, and ripped a piece of baguette in half. "I mean the world just doesn't work like that." I sat there quietly, picked up my own drink, and took a long, slow sip. In the absence of any pushback, she continued, "Like this"—she motioned to the restaurant around us and the food spread out before us—"this is a rarity. I had to put a fake meeting in my calendar to avoid getting caught out! Who takes lunch breaks anymore?"

I said nothing. No response.

"No one!" she said, answering her own question and pointing the other half of the baguette piece at me in a jabbing motion. "And not checking email on the weekend? That just isn't a thing anymore. It just won't work, unless you're choosing to demote yourself." She swallowed her bread, and her expression again softened slightly. "But, Steph, if anyone can make it work, you can. Seriously."

"But what if it was a thing? What if we could choose to work differently? I guess I've just decided that this whole workaholic game isn't a game I want to play anymore."

"Oh you're playing a game, all right—a dangerous game," she said with finality, and raised her glass to mine. "But cheers, I wish you the best of luck."

We eventually finished our lunch, said our goodbyes, and I watched as they dashed across the street and ducked through the revolving doors of my old office tower. I felt unsettled, nervous. They were the first ones I'd been honest with about the scale back.

Were they right? Would I get fired? Was I doing something wrong?

* * *

It got worse.

Later that week at volleyball, Laura, a new player, joined the team and was meeting me for the first time. She also had a lot of questions about the scale back after Luke had announced my experiment to the group as we sat around in the sand.

"I guess I'm just having a hard time with your whole scale back thing," she said. "If I was your boss, I'd be pissed."

I leaned back in the sand, and let my elbows dig in to support me as I gazed out at the lake. This was now becoming a common refrain from everyone who learned about the scale back.

Was *everyone else* really caught up in the productivity-hustle-worth limiting belief that I was trying to distance myself from? The cycle of over-work was so ingrained in our culture, I was starting to doubt my own scale back . . . and yet, I couldn't ignore how incredible I felt.

I looked down at my legs. Everyone had been commenting on my tan, and I'd brushed aside their comments but now, from this angle, I couldn't help but notice the color. They hadn't been this shade since I was a child running around outside all summer. Covered by pantyhose and dress pants, wedged beneath desk tops for every summer of my working life for the last fifteen years had me thinking that I just wasn't a good tanner. Turns out, I just needed to let myself see the sun.

The new girl continued to stare at me. "Sorry, what's your question?" I asked.

"This scale back of yours . . . what's the point? You're just seeing how little work you can do?" Her words were harsh, judgmental. I felt my defenses start to go up and had to remind myself that she'd only met me a couple of hours ago. She knew nothing of my work history, my work ethic. As I started to embrace this new identity—the woman who placed equal priority on life and living with work tasks—I saw how alien this way of living was to so many others as well. We'd been conditioned to accept this hyper-productive approach to work; allowed it to form our identities. It came down to two sides: you were either productive and followed the rules of hyper-productivity, or you were lazy and unambitious.

I wanted to reach out and give her a light shake and ask her: Wouldn't you like to bust free of that false dichotomy? Could you imagine more joy in your life? Or more ease? Wouldn't you like to reclaim your evenings, your weekends? Wouldn't you like to rid yourself of the busy work and focus only on what was essential?

"It means I'm done with hyper-productivity and working for working's sake. I do what's essential to the business, when it's essential for the business. No more, no less."

She shook her head. "Agree to disagree, I suppose," she muttered and packed up her things to head home.

* * *

I started to really question myself when even Cara had concerns.

We were in her cottage kitchen, taking our turn to make breakfast for the group. "It's still something I need to get used to," she said, smiling up at me as she whisked the eggs. "Having you and Luke here, at the same time, together, as a couple."

"Well, you might as well start getting used to it," I shot back with a grin, tossing a tea towel at her as I grabbed the strawberry jam from the pantry.

"So . . .?" she asked, raising one eyebrow as she tapped the fork on the side of the bowl and then tossed it in the sink. "What's happening now with work?"

It was a good question. It had been ramping up even more lately—specifically with the advisors and partners. I was getting more meeting requests, more demands, bigger fundraising targets.

The more tanned I got, and the more outwardly visible my inner relaxation and happiness became, the more demands they seemed to be throwing at me. I felt uneasy around them. Something told me that the more fulfilled I became in my personal life, the more demanding they would become. In their world, if you were relaxed and happy, you were suspect and clearly weren't working hard enough. And yet business was thriving. Conferences and seminars were selling out with big-name speakers; we'd secured a researcher and interns; white papers were in development; and all the fundraising targets were getting hit. Bottom line: I was a success, and working two-thirds the hours.

Cara's question continued to hang between us, her eyes fixed on me. I pulled the strawberry jam into my chest and hunched over it to twist off the lid. As my grip tightened, my knuckles turned white, and I felt my teeth clenching with the effort.

"I think the big bosses are just adjusting to the new me," I said through clenched teeth, and with that the lid pulled free from the jar with a pop. And the pressure released. I passed her the jar. "Yeah . . . they're just getting used to it."

"Well, just be careful," she cautioned. "You don't want them thinking you aren't committed to the work."

"I'm no less committed!" I exclaimed. "I think I'm actually producing better work, I'm just not working as many hou—" I stopped myself mid-sentence, as my words seemed to be going somewhat unheard. Her brow still creased with worry. "Okay, okay," I said in resignation. "I'll be careful."

* * *

While everyone around me seemed to be questioning the scale back and my life choices, Luke and I were on the same page: life was meant to be lived. I had found someone who wanted to seek out new and fun experiences, and—perhaps what I found most interesting of all—he didn't overidentify with his work. It was just one of the many different things he had going on in his life.

That weekend, we were heading to his parents' farm to spend some time with them and also head over to his sister's place for a dinner party. I was eager to leave the pavement, asphalt, and skyscrapers of downtown Toronto behind, and sit on the porch, walk through the barn, and take in the landscape of endless rolling fields. In his hometown, green space dominated, and the physical structures merely dotted the landscape.

I thought back to the conversations I'd had that past week with Jen and Michelle, Laura, and Cara. As I continued with this new lifestyle, one thing was becoming clear: it was rare to find a person with a neutral—let alone supportive—response.

As Luke and I drove to the farm, I shared snippets from the conversations. "Laura thinks I'm not working hard enough, Michelle is convinced I'm going to get fired, and even Cara's concerned," I said, shaking my head.

Luke flashed a sideways smile. "Remember: selective caring," he replied and placed one hand down on my knee and gave it an affectionate squeeze. I gave him a conspiratorial smile and turned to the window to watch the world whizz by.

He gets me, I thought to myself. *And right now, he may be the only one.*

And this was a good thing because, lately, it felt as though the big scale back was under siege. I understood that I was going against the accepted norm for those who considered themselves ambitious. But I was also taken aback at the judgment. Was what I was doing really that radical? And then that little squeak of doubt started to edge its way in. *Was it possible that I was, in fact, becoming lazy?*

I just wanted to find the "and" in it all—I believed I could be ambitious *and* successful *and* operate at a slower, deliberate pace.

I was hoping the visit to the farm and dinner with Luke's sister would help me push all the doubt aside and relax. It started out promising. I now knew most of the people there, but there were a few strangers.

In this case, a couple. The woman, Jane, was quiet and somewhat shy. Her husband, Rob, was louder and more opinionated—already commenting on the approach to cooking the baked potatoes on the barbeque.

I sat next to Jane and we sipped away at our drinks. She got a little chattier with each sip, and she really came to life when talking about her ultimate Frisbee league. Oh, how she loved that league. She'd been playing for years, but for the last two seasons, there were fewer and fewer games. People were becoming less available. At the end of a busy work week, she shared, she was feeling drained and lethargic and had nothing left to give. Then she interrupted her own storytelling: "Wow, this is just making me realize how drained I am at work. I've been working longer and longer hours, which means less and less time for the things I love."

YES!

I took it as an opening. I told her all about the scale back. The pursuit of working in a way that resonated with my own pace and style. Of not buying in to this culture of twelve-plus hour workdays being honorable and the hallmark of success. Of listening to my natural rhythms and how they enabled me to slow down and see what was *really* important. The part of me that recognized that busier wasn't necessarily better. That sleep deprivation meant nothing about commitment to the project, but actually disrespect for the project, as it almost certainly guaranteed that the project wouldn't benefit from the best of my thinking.

She was hooked on every word, nodding, virtually punching the air in agreement. We moved to the dinner table and sat across, facing one another. It was then that her husband joined the table and sat next to her. She turned excitedly to him. "Rob, this is Stephanie. We were just talking about this thing she's doing this summer—"

"Oh, the scale back?" Brett piped in, smiling. "Isn't it awesome?"

"Scale back? What scale back?" Chloe interjected, jokingly punching my arm. "How do I not know this?"

Five sets of eyes were on me, waiting for me to share, and give an update on the book. Emboldened by my conversation with Jane, I dove in with passion. Sharing my thoughts, feelings, and observations. I talked about understanding my constitution, slowing down and listening to myself, paying attention to my own natural rhythms, and parting ways with the work-addiction lifestyle I'd been hooked into for way too long. I spoke about how happy, relaxed, and joyful I felt. Brett raised a glass in agreement; Luke joined in with his own observations and beliefs, while Jane's eyes danced with a blend of joy and mischief, and Chloe asked a lot of questions.

Rob, however, appeared to be sitting in a rotisserie oven—his face a deep red and a line of sweat beaded across his forehead. When he spoke, it was a stern and heavy rebuttal: "The world runs on hard work. Without those of us who work hard, nothing would get done! What you're describing is just lazy and irresponsible. Mortgages have to get paid. Jobs need to get done. And a work ethic is important."

The table went quiet. Glasses were lowered and placed on the table. Gazes fell to plates, and cutlery became objects of fascination.

I exchanged a look with Luke and felt empowered. Five months ago, a reaction like Rob's would have floored me and left me retreating, shrugging my shoulders, and silently disagreeing with him. But after everything I'd experienced this summer—including the success I'd had working significantly fewer hours—I wasn't about to stay quiet.

I spoke about the space I was creating in my calendar, about movement, and quiet time. Less "doing" and more "being." I could see Rob's shoulders tense with every word I uttered until he eventually interjected: "So you're basically slacking off. You know what you're 'scaling back' means? It means that someone else is going to have to pick up the slack and do everything it is you're now *not* doing." His face was reddening and he was visibly agitated. "I'm that guy. I'm always the one making up for everyone else's laziness."

With those words, I softened. I knew what it was like to be the one picking up the slack, or being overly responsible for work tasks. Wasn't that exactly how I'd been living before the scale back? As he turned to say something to his wife, I took the opportunity to push myself back from the table. I gently folded the napkin on my lap and placed it on the charger plate in front of me and slipped away, beelining for the bathroom. I needed to pause, to step away.

I stepped into the bathroom. There was no hiding as the fluorescent light beamed from above, highlighting every worry line creasing my forehead.

So you're just working less? And you're okay with that? The words from the volleyball conversation joined the chorus in my mind. *You're going to get fired.* Michelle's words served as closing argument.

I felt my breath catch as the words kept circling in my mind. I ran my hands under cold water as I stared at my own reflection. *Am I becoming lazy? Am I a giant flake? Am I just not tough enough? Is this scale back a huge mistake?*

I thought about the past week. About the space I'd created to get outside, walk the boardwalk, cook a healthy homemade meal. Space for three yoga classes and evening volleyball. I also thought about the deals I'd closed and the money I'd raised this week. I looked younger than I had in years. I had muscle tone again, my eyes looked vibrant and rested. I felt better than I'd ever felt. Happier, joyful, healthy.

If this was wrong, I didn't want to be right.

I was becoming someone new. And while I couldn't yet define her, I knew who she was *not*. And Rob epitomized that. He wasn't the person I wanted to sit next to at the dinner party. He was high-strung. Stressed. Work was his only topic of conversation. How many times had I been that person? It wasn't who I wanted to be. There had to be a better way.

They'd all dispersed from the table when I'd surfaced from the bathroom. We left the dinner party an hour later. As we walked from the truck to the farmhouse, Luke looked at me and put a hand on my shoulder and pulled me into him, "That Rob . . . what a dud!"

I burst out laughing. *Dud.* Yes. I thought of Rob and his frustration. I couldn't help but wonder if he, too, shared some of the limiting beliefs I'd held since childhood. I may not have been so vocal, but how many times had I felt the same way as Rob? I was ready to commit to this new version of myself—regardless of what the Robs of this world (including my former self) thought. I was on to something. Something good.

NAVIGATING THE PUSHBACK

By now you might be getting to the point in the process where people will really start to notice changes. They may start commenting, reacting, or maybe even complaining or pushing back against the changes you are making. This can be a painful process at times, especially if people you love are pushing back.

When Luke and I started spending more of our weekends at Cara's cottage, I can't tell you how many people were resistant, angry, or at the very least bothered, by this change in my life. Which made sense. The beautiful northern retreat, that brought me so much peace, restoration, and creativity also placed me over two hours away from my friends and family. I wasn't as available as I used to be. And that was difficult for loved ones to understand. It was really tough to feel like I was upsetting and disappointing people I cared about, yet I knew this new lifestyle best served who I wanted to be and how I wanted my life to feel.

People in your life—including those you care about—will react. Part of deepening self-awareness and being a decent human in the world (in my opinion) is being able to take feedback. So what do you do when the feedback you are receiving on your new life changes are negative? When those you love are upset? How can you stand firm in your new belief structure *and* be mindful of the impact on those you love and respect?

Identify whose opinions actually matter. Let's be honest: not everyone has your best interests at heart; and not everyone is invested in your personal growth and evolution. As you're embarking on personal and professional changes in your life, get very clear about whose opinions *actually* matter to you. Brené Brown, author of many of my all-time favorite books (you'll find them in the *Resources* section at the end of this book), suggests using a square piece of paper (small enough that it can fit in your wallet) and writing down the names of the people whose feedback you value and respect. The criteria for including them on your square? You can trust them to hold your best interest in mind *and* to hold you to account and in integrity. I suggest creating a square list for different areas of your life, as the people may differ for each category.

Feedback is someone else's opinion and experience—it is not absolute truth. Tara Mohr, author of *Playing Big*, advises mentally distinguishing between feedback and truth. Sometimes we take feedback from other people as absolute truth when, in fact, it is their experience or opinion. It is their perception—an experience and perception that is true *for them*. Remember that we each perceive a situation through our own unique lens—which is influenced by our core (sometimes limiting) beliefs, personality patterns, and lived experience.

When you receive input and feedback from others:

- Consider the source—are they one of your "square" people?

- Consider their perspective—how might your changes be impacting them and influencing their reaction? How might their comments be a result of their own conditioning, belief structure, and personality patterns?
- Be honest with yourself about the impact—have you had an unintended impact? Hurt someone unintentionally?
- Choose your response—you may consider an apology if you've had an unintended impact. You might share your bigger vision to help them better understand why you're making changes. Perhaps you need to restate a boundary that you've already stated, with some additional context.

The source, perspective, and impact will all determine the response, as well as how much you choose to share or disclose.

YOUR VALUES

Have you ever given conscious thought to your own personal values? That is, those things that are most important to you, that guide your decisions? When we think about values,often the first words that come to mind are "family," "respect," and "integrity." Which words spring to mind for you?

You may have gone your whole life without explicitly stating the values that guide your decision-making. But just because they are operating unconsciously under the surface, doesn't mean they aren't shaping and influencing your day-to-day experience.

I want you to get very intentional and deliberate—*conscious*—of your values, so that they can serve as a handy decision-making criteria when you're facing choices—be they big or small choices—every day.

First, I want you to brainstorm your top values. To help you to do this, think about times in your life when you have felt at your absolute *best*. What themes do you see? How might those themes inform your values and what matters most to you? You can also consider times when you felt at your *worst*. What themes do you see? What values were getting trampled on in those situations?

Once you have your themes and list of words, start to pare the list down. Maybe you can group some of them into themes and come up with one word that can represent the cluster. Maybe some feel much more important than others. I want you to try to narrow the list down to three or four values. (Note: The worksheet at the end of this chapter will support you in doing this work. For sample worksheets and responses, visit stephaniewoodward.com/resources.)

Next, I want you to dig a little deeper. For each of those three or four values, I want you to:

- Describe what these value words mean to you exactly. If you value "family," what does that mean to *you, specifically?* Does family trump everything else in your life? Does it mean that family dinner every night is protected time? Is it your immediate family or does it include your extended family?

- Define what a ten out of ten would look like. If you were fully living into that value, what would it look and feel like?

- Define a zero out of ten. When you are not living into that value at all, what would it look and feel like?

- Finally, consider how you'd rank that value *right now*, given your current circumstances. Which ones are you fully honoring and living into? And which ones need improvement?

In my own life, "balance" is one of my top values. The time of scale back represented a ten out of ten, whereas my life prior to the scale back represented a zero. Approaching my values *consciously*, I check in with myself often, to gauge how well (or not) I am living into each one. When I check in on my value of "balance" now, my assessment usually falls between a seven and a ten. That is an acceptable range for me. Lower than a seven has me making adjustments in my life to bring myself back into my acceptable range.

Think about this for yourself and your own values: what is an acceptable range? And how will you check in with your values on regular basis?

YOUR LIFE PIE

To help you stay connected to your new belief structure, the changes you're making, and your values, I'd like you to create a visual that you can use as a practical tool to keep this alive for yourself. The Coaches Training Institute introduced me to the "life pie" and it's a tool I use for myself—and with clients—often. It's a straightforward, practical, and simple way to stay connected to your commitments to yourself and your life.

You can use a good old-fashioned piece of paper and some colored pens or markers, or you can use an online tool like Mural, Miro, Whimsical, or Canva to bring this to life. Start by placing the values you identified, one in each corner of the page. In the center, draw a large circle.

Next, think about all the important "categories" of your life. Mine include: relationship, career, health, hobbies, parenting, friends, family/extended family, homemaking, finances. Your image will end up looking something like this (though make it as creative and colorful as you wish!):

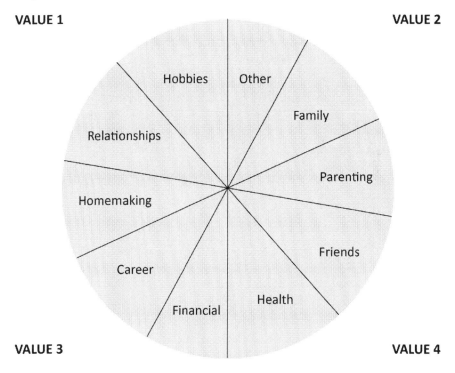

VALUE 1   **VALUE 2**

Hobbies   Other

Family

Relationships

Parenting

Homemaking

Friends

Career

Health

Financial

VALUE 3   **VALUE 4**

For *each* life pie category, ask yourself:

- What does *great* look like? What would a ten out of ten look like? During the scale back, I felt the healthiest I'd ever been. I was working out regularly, eating healthy food, and getting plenty of sleep. Every ailment of mine disappeared. The scale back remains my definition of ten out of ten in the "health" category.

- What does *unacceptable* look like? What would constitute a zero out of ten? When I was dehydrated and essentially unconscious on the couch prior to the scale back, I'd reached my lowest point in the "health" category. It remains my definition of zero out of ten for the health category.

- What does the *bare minimum* look like? For the "health" category, my bare minimum includes a yoga class a week, at least two 30-minute breaks in my work day, and a good helping of fruits and vegetables every day.

- What ranking would you give this category *right now, in its current state*? My ranking on this category typically fluctuates from a seven to ten (which places me above my bare minimum).

Capture your notes directly on your diagram, if it's large enough, or write these notes separately. This is incredibly valuable information because once you've worked your way through these questions, you now have your *ideal* (ten out of ten), what's *unacceptable* (zero out of ten), and your *bare minimum* for each category. This serves as a visual depiction of where you need to prioritize your focus. If you have categories that are below your *bare minimum* ranking, you may want to prioritize attention and action in service of those categories first.

DERAILERS

Finally, for each of your life pie categories, I want you to identify situations or circumstances that have you slip back into old habits. These are your *derailers*, and I want you to be really conscious of them so that you notice when they show up to throw you off your success. For example, one of my derailers is when someone I respect or care about asks me to do something—just about anything—for them or with them. Regardless of how it impacts my value of "balance" or my "health" life pie category, I *always* want to say yes. "Yes" is my default response. I am now very conscious of this derailer, and as a result, I pause before responding to requests, or if it's an in-person or in-the-moment request, I very rarely say yes on the spot. I buy myself time to provide an answer. And if I know it's a "no," I (hopefully graciously) say so.

You have now identified your values, assessed your life pie categories, and identified your derailers—*let this become a practice in your life*. These are really practical tools that will support you in living a life of *conscious productivity*—a life truly of your own design. In the next—and final—chapter, we'll bring it all together to set you up for success (on your own terms).

WORKSHEET

IDENTIFY YOUR VALUES

Think of three times in your life when you felt at your absolute best:

Experience 1:

Experience 2:

Experience 3:

Review your experiences above. What themes do you see? How do those themes inform your values (what matters most to you)?

Think of three times in your life when you felt at your absolute *worst*:

Experience 1:

Experience 2:

Experience 3:

Review your experiences above. What themes do you see? How do those themes inform your values (what matters most to you)?

Pare down your list! Identify your top 3-4 values.

WORKSHEET

IDENTIFY YOUR DERAILERS

For each of your life pie categories, identify situations or circumstances that have you slip back into old (bad) habits. These are your derailers.

e.g., Life pie category: Health

Situation 1: taking my computer to the couch after 7 p.m.

Situation 2: starting my day by looking at my inbox.

Situation 3: I say yes by default when someone asks for something.

For each of your derailers, identify what you will do, instead, in those situations.

e.g., I will leave my computer in another room; I will swap out my phone for an alarm clock and start my day with a walk; I will pause and buy myself time before saying "yes" or "no" to a request.

CHAPTER 10

THE BIG SCALE BACK

One of the most popular topics in my coaching conversations—across gender, positions, industries, and generations—is work–life balance. What does it mean to have "balance"? Is it even possible? You can find many different perspectives and approaches to finding balance and harmony in your life.

Sometimes I think we can (falsely) equate work–life balance with being able to do what we want, when we want. At least, that's the resistance I get from some senior leaders who are fearful when they hear that employees want more work–life balance.

As we step into this topic I want to be clear: work–life balance is not being able to do what you want, when you want, all the time. Honestly, I don't think that would lead to successful outcomes in either your personal life or your professional life. I believe it's about switching from *I can do what I want when I want all the time* to *I am setting up the conditions for myself to be able to give my best across the areas of life that really matter to me, so that I can feel fulfilled over the course of my life.*

WHAT'S YOUR BALANCE?

Here's my take: Your life pie—grounded in your values and your definition for each category—serves as a foundation for you to define what "balance" and "success" mean for you in your life. **YOU are the only one who can define balance and success for yourself.** You've defined *ideal, unacceptable,* and *bare minimum* levels—those provide you with a range for what's acceptable as you move through different circumstances in your life.

There might be times when you are lying closer to the ideal in certain categories, and other times when you are sitting closer to the bare minimum. That's okay. The alarm bells go off when you fall into the *unacceptable* zone—this is when you've entered unacceptable territory, and it's time to make some changes.

PHASES

There are also *phases* in your life—and remind yourself of that. As a new parent, life may seem exceptionally skewed to the parenting category. During this phase, the hobbies and health categories may tread dangerously close to unacceptable levels. Be compassionate with yourself during these phases. Bring them into your awareness *consciously.* Simply by vocalizing this to yourself can help bring peace, compassion, and deeper fulfillment to your experience: "Oh, I'm feeling unfulfilled right now because I haven't worked out in weeks, and I haven't had a moment to myself to read. It's been all work and caretaking because

I've been caught up with this little nugget." (Cue your sideways glance at your child.) Consciously identifying what's going on for you is a critical part of living a balanced, fulfilled life. You'd be amazed at the sense of relief you might feel by simply *correctly articulating* what is causing you to feel off balance. It also helps you to identify next steps or action you can take to reintroduce some balance.

A phase of life is just that—a phase.

ENVIRONMENTS

In addition to phases of life, there are also *environments* to consider. Throughout my working life, there were organizations and work environments where—despite my efforts to place boundaries while honoring my responsibilities and accountabilities—it simply wouldn't work. In those cases, my values (and the acceptable range in my "career" life pie category) were completely out of alignment with those of the organization or specific senior executives who wielded a tremendous amount of influence. Once I was able to articulate my values and unacceptable life pie ranges, clearly to myself, the career decisions became obvious—this workplace culture, this organization, and this style of leadership was simply not aligned with my values or, in other cases, *simply not up to my standards.*

Notice how that statement depersonalizes it. It's not about anyone being good or bad. It's about finding *alignment.* Sometimes your personal values might be at odds with the values of your organization, boss, or colleagues. Depending on the level of misalignment, it may be time to look elsewhere. As one individual, you likely won't change the values of the organization, leadership team, or your colleagues. The key is finding a working environment that aligns with your values in the first place.

Conscious productivity is about knowing and owning what life balance looks like for you, being honest about it, and identifying roles and work that allow you to live into your version of balance *while also* holding up your end of the deal: honoring your responsibilities and accountabilities at work.

Work–life balance, integration, and harmony isn't one-sided. It isn't just about what works for your life. It's also about meeting your responsibilities and accountabilities, which is why I asked you to do such a deep dive on your constitution, and identify your strengths and your "what I know for sure" list, so that you can be honest with yourself about the types of roles and responsibilities that align well with *your* desired lifestyle, *your* constitution, and *your* strengths.

That, to me, is the secret to work–life harmony, and living a life of fulfillment.

Be ready to be unpopular and to make tough decisions.

Here's what often remains unspoken, but I want to make it explicit: living your life by your own design will likely create disruption in your life. You may need to disappoint others. **The key, going forward, is not disappointing yourself.**

In my work settings, no one—*no one*—cared about my health. Now, if you were to ask them outright, no one would admit to wishing me ill-health. I don't think anyone is that spiteful or ill-intentioned. But they did want me to be a workhorse without complaint. They *did* want me available at all hours. They *did* expect me to drop everything and anything at a moment's notice. This wasn't my perception; this was truth based on their observable actions, requests, and responses.

I'm not alone in this. As you read this, what is *your* reaction? Are you feeling shunned or reprimanded for seeking some semblance of balance between your work and personal life? If you're a leader reading this, what are your *actions* saying to your employees? You may not be wishing them ill-will or ill-health, but what are your observable actions, requests, and responses saying?

Critical and foundational to this, of course, is accountability. And that's what I always kept top-of-mind during the scale back. I had a responsibility to my employer—and I delivered. I never shirked responsibilities. I never dropped the ball on objectives. **Balance, freedom, and autonomy require accountability and a sense of responsibility.** This isn't about ducking out of responsibilities. It's about gaining clarity on responsibilities and outcomes—and prioritizing those so that you can meet your responsibilities *and* enjoy the rest of your life as well.

The issue becomes—when there are often too few people and too few dollars—the responsibility list becomes unreasonable. Managing an appropriate amount of workload is a leader's key responsibility. There will always be enough work to fill evenings and weekends, but is it appropriate to expect and demand that? The research overwhelmingly suggests that it isn't. As you begin putting your new definitions of success and balance into practice, you may have some tough decisions to make about who you work for—both at the organizational and individual level.

Others may not be on the same journey as you.

Throughout the scale back, I realized that my new habits and actions—connected to my newly forming identity—were crashing up against the habits and actions of others. While I was doing the work to untangle myself from hyper-productivity, others weren't. Not only *weren't* they, they had no desire to. They weren't on a scale back, nor do I think they were interested in one. If I was changing and they weren't, what then?

This will happen as you connect to a newly forming identity. You may crash up against others who are living in their own beliefs and conditioned patterns and behaviors. And they may have no interest in changing themselves or embracing your new habits and actions. After all, you're the one changing, not them.

As you move through personal transformation and change, you'll have to make some critical decisions along the way. Which relationships are most critical to you? Those are the ones you need to invite in on your journey. Share context, be specific about the changes they'll see, and ask for the support you need. You may choose to invite feedback from them along the way, as well.

You'll also need to identify the people and relationships that aren't critical, and you may need to gently, or firmly, part ways. This won't necessarily be easy or comfortable, but it is often necessary when embarking on big change. If your values now clash with those of your organization, your team, or your boss, *they may not change*. And it's not their responsibility to change, necessarily. So to honor your new values, it may be time to look for a new role within a new organization where your values more closely align.

This may be true with other colleagues and friendships and other relationships. You're not in the business of changing other people; you're in the business now of living into your truth, honoring the values that feel true to you and are in line with what you desire for your life while honoring your own constitution. This might mean parting ways with those you are now out of alignment with.

* * *

As I continued through the summer focusing on my essential commitments, while also prioritizing down time, I noticed some significant changes. I was stronger and healthier than I'd ever been, thanks to extra time to prepare healthy meals, actually get to the gym, and get outside for real, consistent movement, and strength training.

I was also happier than ever, feeling like my life had achieved some balance. I had a wonderful relationship *and* a good job. For a moment in time that summer, I truly believed I could—and in fact, did—have it all. I thought I'd cracked the code on the whole balance thing. I was prioritizing the essentials, putting a cap on work hours, and taking the time to rest, have fun, and *be* in the rest of my life.

So I felt confident going into the fall. I had a winning formula, and things were going well on all fronts. Luke and I had decided to take an extended weekend getaway to New York. I'd be taking two days away from work, but everything was in good shape. I still had negative associations with vacation time from previous roles—remember the "drowning" incident? That experience followed me into every role after that one. I reminded myself of my successes, *and* I'd updated my advisors that week about all the goings-on, in preparation for my time off.

As the plane taxied away from the gate, I went to turn my phone to Airplane Mode when I noticed a new email. I read it, stunned, and then reread it, just to be sure I had read it correctly the first time: *Hey, Steph, don't panic. We'll chat through this when you get back. Obviously we won't do anything about this unless it makes sense to do so. Enjoy the rest of your vacation.*

Attached to the email was a four-page document that I was able to scan and get the gist of pretty quickly. It was a proposal by a prominent man to replace me and introduce a new leadership team, including placing himself at the helm.

And they'd forwarded me this email the Friday morning of my four-day vacation.

I felt stress course through me, a shiver ran down my spine, and my heart started beating faster. I did a quick online search to read up on the man who'd sent the proposal. He had very limited related experience, and he was significantly older than me. Other than connections, he had no business suggesting himself for this role.

The fact that the advisors had forwarded such a ludicrous proposal to me also left me reeling.

Be careful—you'll get fired. The words of warning from so many people played on repeat in my mind. I quickly cycled through my objectives in my mind: I'd nailed them all. There was no objective reason for my performance to be in question; except for the fact that I was no longer available 24/7.

Was that at the root of this? Was this a way to reassert dominance and control? To put me in my place? To remind me that I was replaceable?

I'd always been the worker who'd said yes, had no boundaries, put work before everything else. Is this what happened to others when they attempted to have a life? Was this the way the work world worked, and I'd just been oblivious because I'd always been deferential, subservient, and complicit with workaholic norms?

Looking back on this now, I absolutely do believe it was a warning. A message to say I was treading on thin ice. With this particular work—where there was SO much to get done, more than was possible for one person to complete, and so many advisors, all with competing priorities—there was always *something* that *someone* could say wasn't getting done. When I had been working myself to the bone—and my health had paid the price—everyone commended me for working that hard. Working myself to exhaustion was equated with ambition and work ethic.

Coming back to that email (I won't leave you in suspense), I spoke with the advisors, directly and point blank, listing, one by one, my concerns with the proposal of this prominent man to replace me: a simple Google search revealed this formerly influential individual had a questionable reputation; he had a lack of understanding of our business, as demonstrated by several contradictions in his proposal; and I continued to list all the reasons why this man—with minimal related experience—should not be able to propose to replace me and have it be entertained. I expressed my disappointment and concern.

The subject was dropped. And we resumed business as usual. Or so they thought. But that one action had done it for me: I knew I was done doing business this way. There was a values clash that was irreconcilable in my mind.

In my consulting business now, I see this all the time. High turn-over rates; high performers leaving "for a better opportunity" or "a corporate culture that is more of a fit." This is all code for what I, too, felt in that moment. I decided that to fix the problem—to convince others who demonstrated no investment in me as a human—was a battle I wasn't interested in fighting. I'd simply go elsewhere.

And this is what is whispered to me in coaching calls all day, every day: feelings of being treated as less than human, as a cog, as a commodity, to be burned through and replaced when needed.

Understanding your employees as humans, and what balance means to them, is the key to retaining top talent.

* * *

It was one thing to make the decision that I was done and that I was going to leave the role. It was another thing to actually *leave*. Looking back now, I would tell myself: *The future is bright! Leave!* But in the moment, I was having a very human response: I was scared and I was confused.

Ever felt that way about career change?

Based on the hundreds and hundreds of hours I've spent on the phone with clients contemplating career change, I feel quite confident that the answer is yes.

Financial responsibilities, concern about "what if it's worse somewhere else?" or "I know I don't want *this*, but I don't know what I *do* want." By the time we're contemplating career change, we tend to be so exhausted, frustrated, or fed up that we've lost some of our mental processing power.

That's where I was at: angry, frustrated, exhausted. But I was also determined and resolute. I was done being at the mercy of other's beliefs that were at odds with my values and newly formed beliefs. Because that was what my work life had become: working for a series of individuals who had deep-seated beliefs about productivity, worth, ambition, and hustle. Takes one to see one. And the more I started to untangle myself from those limiting beliefs, the more I could spot them in others. I wanted to work with others who were disentangling themselves from those beliefs *and* who were doing inspiring work in the world.

I wanted to help others—individuals, leaders, and teams—disentangle themselves from these limiting beliefs. To honor responsibilities, be accountable for outcomes, *and* create space for fulfillment beyond work productivity.

At this point, I didn't know *how* I was going to do that. But I knew what I needed to help me figure it out: Luke and Stone Lake.

* * *

The parking lot was nothing more than a forest clearing scattered with gravel at the end of the private country road. It was maintained, but to be used by, hikers and local cottage owners only. The truck bounced slightly as it crunched the gravel underneath and slowed to a stop. Ours was the only vehicle in the lot—it was early April—so the cottagers had yet to arrive and the hikers were likely waiting for the warmer weather. It was almost a year to the day we had first met, and Luke and I had returned to Stone Lake. Only this time, instead of canoeing to Cara's cottage, we'd decided to hike in via the Wilderness Trail.

As I stepped out of the truck, I was struck by the lack of chill in the air. Above, I could hear the icicles dripping their way to oblivion, and the snow beneath my feet was the consistency of a slushy at the local fairground. Melt water pooled around my boots as my feet sank into the mud at the edge of the lot. I wiggled them around a bit, enjoying the satisfying slurp of the suction as they moved in and out of the muck.

It was equal parts whim, practicality, and adventure that had us trekking the expansive forest trail this weekend. When we'd asked Cara for access to her cottage, we thought we'd be able to boat the perimeter, knowing that the lake wouldn't be frozen enough to cross on foot, nor clear of ice to have a direct clear path across in the boat. I'd imagined us paddling around the edges, hugging the shoreline, with Luke perhaps needing to stand every now and then to nudge a floating ice chunk out of the way while impersonating an Italian gondola driver, serenading me with an operatic falsetto.

As the weekend drew closer, though, and the temperatures hovered around freezing, even the perimeter seemed an unlikely path. There was only one other way in. The cottage properties backed on to thousands of acres of conservation land. And snaking through those wildlands—through rivers, up and down hilly terrain, and marked only by the odd brushstroke of white paint on tree trunks—was the Wilderness Trail.

Luke stepped out and in front of the truck, then, fiddled with the straps on his backpack as he turned to face me. Around his neck was a whistle and clipped to his belt on the right was his axe; on the left hip, his machete. Strung across his chest was a chainsaw connected to a self-made sash of ratchet straps. Whistle, axe, machete, chainsaw. "To be used in precisely that order if we're attacked by a bear," he'd said that morning, casually, earnestly, as he spooned the last of the Vector cereal into his mouth. Looking at him now, I smiled at my mountain of a man who stood before me.

It was a reminder of what lay ahead of us: four hours of wilderness, animals, ridges, rivers, and rocks. Looking up at the aged pine tree in front of me, hammered in to the trunk, just above my eye level was the little diamond-shaped trail sign, bold black font jumping from the highlighter yellow background: "WILDERNESS TRAIL" it read. And beneath that: "WARNING: EXPERIENCED HIKERS ONLY!" Its all-capped letters barking out their warning.

We were not outdoorsy people, at least not by traditional standards. We didn't camp or do daylong excursions, and we were certainly not avid hikers. This wasn't about the challenge of the hike. The hike was simply the means required to get to the weekend living we craved—remote, quiet, without pretense—where time stood still, or at least slowed down.

I closed my eyes and exhaled.

The mental weight of the past week at work—many barbells' worth of threats, demands, and unknowns—shifted then. From fear to resolve. I had decisions to make; I needed a plan.

"Ready there, trailblazer?" Luke's smile was infectious as he nudged my arm and turned me around to tighten one of my pack straps, tapping my back gently when he was done.

It brought me back to the present. *This hike. This moment. Just be here, with Luke, and the forest. The answers will come.*

My brain muscles softened and relaxed, while my back and shoulders tensed, coming alive to do what was actually necessary and needed now for survival. As though sixty pounds were oozing from my brain to the pack on my back. Sixty pounds of worry and abstract thoughts about deadlines and threats displaced to sixty pounds of water canteens, a cast iron pan, and forty-eight hours' worth of food provisions.

And there was Luke: all whistle, axe, machete, and chainsaw. At the ready, always prepared. We'd now be climbing, wading, and hacking our way through to an un-winterized cottage on the other side of the lake. No running water or amenities. Boiling lake water to drink, chopping wood for heat, and eating over the campfire.

As we crossed over from the gravel lot to take our first steps on the mud-and-slush-packed Wilderness Trail, Luke stepped out in front, and taking a quick glance at the GPS device in his left hand, he pointed up to the rocky ridge looming before us—ice-slicked in some spots, wet and muddy in others. The forest canopy shielded us from the sunlight. This was the start of the trail. Without pause or words, he was off, hiking a zig-zagging pattern up the ridge, dodging branches and twigs, side-stepping wet patches, and doing a few gratuitous swings of his machete to clear some of the brush. I followed, literally stepping into his footprints, weaving my way along his zig-zag path on a thirty-second delay.

One foot in front of the other. Testing the stability of the rocks with my big toe before planting my foot. Watching for ice, for mud. My feet finding the contours of his footprints, and sinking in gladly. Allowing myself to be led, trusting myself to follow well. A line of light—like a laser cutting through the path—streaked across my boot. I paused and looked up at the smallest patch of sky peeking between the forest rooftop of evergreen tips. Up ahead, the sound of Luke through the leaves as he continued the zig-zag. And I exhaled.

There was nowhere I would rather be.

An hour in, I pushed the arms of my fleece back past my elbows, wanting the cool humid air to curl around my forearms. The trees were denser, thicker in this particular part of the trail. It was filled with evergreens, their needles craved some touch and attention, I imagined, after a winter of hibernation and snow cover. Gently pushing some of their branches aside, ducking under others, I felt the tingle and scratch of the branch tips on my arms and cheeks. With every graze, they reminded me that, I too, was craving their touch and attention after a winter of hibernation and snow cover.

We approached the beaver pond—our first resting spot—an hour and a half in. The beaver pond was true to its name, a wide expanse of shallow water, speckled with the crisscrossing wood of beaver dams. The ice cover of the pond was now no more than a smattering of icy, slushy peaks and valleys dotting the pond, the water was breaking through and around them where it could.

I reached for the water bottle clipped to Luke's pack and brought it to my mouth. As I sipped, I felt quenched in a way I had never felt before. Satisfying a thirst I hadn't realized was so deep. This water seemed to carry with it the forest air, the slowing of time, and the northern tranquility. An elixir brewed up by these Wilderness forces specifically for my soul. I could almost feel my cells dancing—emboldened—savoring and soaking up every drop.

The next incline screamed out with instability. Its ground was soggy in some places, slick where the runoff was flowing freely, and saturated in others where the water had pooled in the crevices created by the intersection of tree roots and rocks. I stomped, planted, and wiggled my leading foot with every step, testing the ground before I shifted my weight. The repetitive thud of each step was cathartic: an outlet for my pent-up anger and aggression from the week, as a scene began playing out in my mind.

I was penning a resignation, and when I submitted it, it wasn't accepted. I imagined myself pushing back, negotiating, working through the conflict in my mind.

The scene was interrupted then and went to black as Luke called out from below, "Watch that one!" He was pointing at a stone in front of me as I approached a short, but steep, decline to the river's edge. He was about twenty feet ahead, standing at an angle almost perpendicular to me. His right shoulder pointed toward where we were heading, his left shoulder pointing at me. "It's deceivingly steady looking, but it's not."

His warning came too late. My foot slid on the rock, and the mossy carpet slid with it. I reached out for the branch in front of me to steady myself. The branch looked thick, strong, and I grabbed it, just as my hip started to fold under me. For a moment, the branch caught my fall. Long enough for my muscles to unclench and my mind to relax. And then it snapped, and completely unprepared, I went straight down, landing slightly sideways, my hip bone colliding with a rock and absorbing the weight of the fall.

Are you kidding me?! I grumbled under my breath and at the branch, which was still in my hand, the top of it curving up and back, as though throwing itself back in a fit of laughter. Luke was looking up at me with a half-smile, knowing I was more shocked than hurt, and having likely heard me cursing the branch and then calling out an emphatic and heartfelt "take that!" as I whipped it down the hill. I waved away any concern, signaling "onward" with the gesture, pulled myself back up, and brushed off the leaves and other pieces of the forest floor clinging to my pants.

Stay present. The answers will come.

* * *

Four hours, twenty-three minutes later—and both of our bodies, by some miracle, uninjured—we sat in the Muskoka chairs on Cara's dock, sipping our wine from oversized plastic wine glasses, while the lake air around us swirled, carrying with it the chirps of the spring peepers, the staccato of the woodpecker, and the lap of the water against the wooden slats. The sky let its lids get heavy as dusk began to fall over the lake. A Canada goose called out, and flew past, its mate a beak's length behind. And a knowing came to me; the surest of knowings.

This is home to me.

Being with the water's ripples, bearing witness to the birds returning home, being with the changing of the season, gazing at the newly forming buds and wondering just when they would decide to join us. Here. Now. This. Us. This was home to me.

And as though I'd said it out loud, Luke turned his glass toward mine, looking from me, out across the lake, and back to me again, he said, "To all this."

We clinked glasses, and my body relaxed. *The answers will come.*

* * *

We walked back out two days later. I'd had time to reflect, pause, and think about my next steps.

I suddenly felt connected, truly, to the ground I was standing on. This is what it is to be human. The corporate hamster wheel back in Toronto wasn't my version of living.

As we stepped into the forest and moved forward on the trail, I knew, there was about to be a new order of things in my life.

* * *

Luke and I were spending yet another weekend at Cara's cottage, though this time, Luke was doing some work on the cottage, building a new set of stairs from the dock to the front deck.

I was in my usual position: screened-in room, lake view, with my writing journal, computer, and assortment of pens and sticky notes. I was jotting down some ideas, when I noticed a canoe pull up to the dock, and the man in the canoe struck up a conversation with Luke. I watched as the man pointed his finger south and made a motion as though to say "further down that way." They spoke for a few minutes, then the man and the canoe left, and Luke walked up to the cottage.

"Well that was interesting," he said, sinking into the couch next to me. "He's seen me doing work around here . . . and he told me to take a look at his cottage with a 'buyer's mind.'"

He wanted Luke to let him know whether the place would need much work before putting it up for sale. We jumped in the boat and headed down to this other cottage to take a look. It was a massive fixer-upper. Virtually everything needed attention, investment, and repair.

We looked at each other, and it was as though the words had already been spoken aloud before we both said, "What if we bought it?"

And just like that, we made the decision to buy a cottage. A teeny tiny fixer-upper on a boat-access lake. A teeny tiny cottage that was going to need a LOT of work. But neither of us cared. Not only did this lake define and shape so much of our early time together, but I truly felt that it had healed me. This land and this water had helped me work through these limiting beliefs and allowed me to disengage and unplug from the world of productivity that had hooked me for so long.

A month later, as I sat next to our own campfire, poking at the burning wood and ashes, I thought of Dad. I thought about all those years I'd spent as a child, teenager, and early adult . . . working so hard, desperate to make him proud. If he were alive, what would he be thinking right now, I wondered. I also realized that this question wasn't coming from a place of wanting his approval or validation, but more out of curiosity. What *had* he thought of my ambition? Of my goals?

I poked at one log, and it disintegrated to ash. Then, it was as though I was understanding my dad in a whole other way. Maybe my dad was his own version of a feminist. As I thought back on what conversations I'd had with him and his odd obsession with career prospects. Never was there a mention of a relationship or marriage or kids. Perhaps he wanted me to be financially independent. Perhaps he wanted me to be on par with men and the boys network that he would have known existed at the time. Perhaps he never wanted me to depend on a man for money. Maybe that's why he placed an over importance on my marks.

I'd never know; but I liked this perspective.

* * *

Dad only knew how to want for me what he'd wanted for himself. He wanted me to be great and have a great life; but he only knew how to define "great" on his own terms. And I'd hung on his every word as a kid, wanting to please, and so I'd taken on his definition of success as my own, rather than writing my own definition.

The man who blocked precisely six times in his calendar every year: each of our birthday mornings, Christmas eve afternoon through to New Year's, and Halloween night. Any other day or time was fair game for work to permeate, overtake, dominate, or creep its way in. Or serve as a subtle hum in the background, distracting him from everything going on right in front of him. It is only now, watching my friends raising their own children and hearing of their childhoods that I realize that not all dads placed work first. Some dads were home for dinner every night; some dads knew the school teachers' names; some dads coached teams; some did drop-offs and pickups; others went for ice cream on a random Tuesday. I never felt that daily adoration that comes from a dad who is in the thick of it with you every day. And now, I was the one who'd been placing work first; the one who'd been missing out on the thick of it every day.

What WAS this past year of scaling back? It had seemed like a fun experiment at the time, but it had become much, much more. There was no turning back now. I was finding pieces of myself every day that had been waiting to be reclaimed.

It seemed I had a choice: stay in this role and go back to my old patterns—or leave.

I picked at the peeling wood on the bench I was sitting on, pulling at a narrow strip, tearing an inch by inch chunk cleanly from the surface. I held it in my hand, really looking at the grain of the wood, and imagined the multiple splinters that made up that little wedge. I looked up from that piece of wood in my hand to the vast expanse of lake flowing out in every direction.

I felt the tears prickling the corners of my eye, and I blinked them back. Work had not only been an accepted priority—it had been THE priority. My oh-so well-intentioned dad had set up a pattern, a belief structure, in my life that I never knew was a structure I could opt out of. It was presented as fact: this was what it was to work. It was to be all-consuming and to be prioritized above all else. That life could be neglected and pushed aside when a deadline loomed or a demand was made.

And now here I was, in an all-consuming role that was demanding more and more of my time while this incredible life was being offered up to me at the same time. A life much better lived when scaled back and unhooked from all the patterns and structures that had been with me since childhood. I poked at the stone with a long, thick branch that was mostly charred at the end, injuries it sustained after my last fireside vigil. And it's only when the tear landed on my hand that I realized I was crying. *I choose my life.*

I stood and reached over to the pile of pine branches next to the pit and tossed one too many into the campfire. The dried sap served as fuel to the flames, their hungry tips lapping and encircling the green of the pine needles as they all twisted and curled in the heat. The fire tripled in height. The flames licked at the needles with ferocity, rendering them ash within minutes.

I tossed another armful of pine branches into the pit, feeding the flames. They curled, licked, and twisted, and the smoke stung my eyes as the needles surrendered, knowing this was the time. Sometimes you need to burn it all down. It was time to surrender this working life I had built. Let it burn down, with the flame lit by my own hand. I trusted that I would rise stronger—and happier—from this ash.

It was time to write my own definition of success.

* * *

It was 6 a.m., and I was wide awake. Outside the cottage window, an oak branch swayed only inches from the glass. I watched it dance through our uncurtained windows. Luke was asleep soundly beside me, peaceful, unstirring.

And it occurred to me then: *I am at peace. Here, now, in this wilderness, next to this man, with a business I am about to build. It was all coming together. All of it.*

I had a sudden urge to shake Luke awake and proclaim: "This is it! Our life exactly as it is—this is what it's all been for!"

But instead, I rolled sideways and tucked my arm under the pillow and propped myself up slightly to face him. Had he opened his eyes, he would've seen a bird's-nest-haired, mascara-smudged face grinning in gratitude of it all. He also would have been startled and likely would have playfully nudged me onto my back so that I wasn't staring at him.

But he didn't open his eyes. And so I could lie there, bird's-nest-haired, mascara-smudged, and grinning way too broadly at the man who came into my life exactly when I was ready for him. For us to build exactly this life.

* * *

I found my journal from when I was just starting the big scale back and uncovered my original checklist:

Move my body. *Check*

Pay the bills. *Check*

Have fun. *Double check.*

Love.

My breath caught at this last one as I looked over at Luke sleeping next to me and in that moment, I took in this past year and everything he had brought into my life.

One giant, bolded, highlighter yellow check.

* * *

So, what happened in the story? What did I do about that role?

Well, I penned a resignation, that's what I did. And I expected a cold sweat to break out or jitters to cramp my fingers and forbid me from hitting send on the letter. But instead, with every keyboard strike, I was injected with an exhilaration.

Am I really doing this? CAN I really do this?!

A year prior, the fear may have tripped me up. But these last two years had changed me. I felt battle weary and beaten up; I felt exhausted and professionally unfulfilled. But I also felt strong. I had survived it all. And not just survived, but thrived. People could say whatever they wanted about my approach, but the results spoke for themselves:

I'd achieved great outcomes and I was proud of what I'd built. At this point, though, I wanted to work in a different way. I trusted the new rhythms I'd found. I really, truly believed in a different approach to work. One that honored my ambition *and* my many other interests and facets of life. Work was only one part of my identity.

I knew what it took for me to operate at my best: strategizing, prioritizing, and proper pacing. Proper pacing meant rest and fun and vacation time *before* I hit a breaking point. As I signed off the final "d" in Woodward—essentially signing off on traditional corporate life—I thought of Dad.

I think you were wrong, Dad, to think there was only one path, one way, for me. To put the striving, the ambition above all else. I didn't need to be molded into a mini-you to be successful. A title—a role—I've learned, does not define who I am. But you were right to push me, to have me recognize what was possible. To reach, to strive, to instill an incredibly strong—and unshakeable—work ethic. I wouldn't be here now, taking this leap having discovered what I truly want, had I not pursued a path that so very challenged my very core and constitution.

I decided I was going to start my own business: Agency to Change. Dedicated to working with those who wanted agency and personal ownership over their own lives. Who wanted to write their own stories as individuals, as leaders, and in whatever roles they found themselves. Those who wanted to live a life of their own design. And leaders who appreciate that every member of their team is an individual with their own drives, motivations, and constitution. Who honors them as a human, and understands that their identity extends well beyond work.

I walked into the cottage. Luke was sitting in the screened-in room, chomping on some summer sausage slices and washing them down with a beer.

"And so it will be," I declared somewhat ceremoniously as I handed him the letter. He read it over, beginning to end, looked up, and smiled without saying a word.

"I can really do this?" I said, more question than declaration. "I'll be okay?" My voice rose several octaves with the second question, as it always did when I was nervous.

He pulled me down on to the couch, and I landed down and partly over him, one leg draped over his, the rest of me resting back against the cushion. He looked me squarely in the eye and said, "Something tells me that you will be more than okay."

There was no dramatic, pumped-up quality to his voice. It was that earnest steadiness, that solidity of his gaze. And I knew it was all going to be okay. More than okay.

* * *

AFTERWORD

I now own my own business, Agency to Change. I am my own boss. And I STILL need to manage my tendency toward overwork and burn-out. Managing and balancing my nervous system. I think this will be ongoing work for me for the rest of my life.

But I'm consciously aware of it.

I pay attention to it.

I now reflect every day, deliberately and consciously, so that I'm making subtle adjustments in my life and to my ways of working, rather than letting unconscious habits and patterns run the show, and eventually creating the need for massive swings and changes. Now it's about checking in, monitoring, and making subtle pivots, adjustments, and swerves as needed. The "refinement" of conscious productivity.

WHAT I LEARNED FROM THE SCALE BACK

When it comes to work, productivity, and ambition, everyone has an opinion. Throughout this entire process of the scale back—heck, my entire career—it was hard *not* to think there was something wrong with me. After all, others were going about their day jobs without question, climbing corporate ladders with glee. They also questioned every career move I made: Why would I leave the security of a corporate role? Why would I abandon a steady salary? Why didn't I feel *grateful* for all the opportunities that had come my way? Didn't I know that work was called "work" for a reason?

Here's what the scale back taught me, and my reflection on my career—and life:

1. *I had been climbing the wrong ladders.* I'd deviated further and further from the two things I knew I loved: the psychology of people and interpersonal dynamics.

2. *I'd let others define my path.* Whether it was parents, bosses, friends, or well-meaning humans in just about any other area of my life, I'd let their vision of what *they* thought was best for me overshadow what *I* knew was best for me.

3. *I had been working against my constitution.* I'm a creative and relational person. I crave depth. I love interpersonal dynamics. I create space for discussion, dialogue, and creativity. That spaciousness runs at a slower pace than the norm. Slower doesn't mean *wrong*—in fact, it's often exactly what's needed for the best outcomes.

4. *I didn't know how to check in with myself.* The signs were all there. Always. I spent the majority of my life looking outside of myself for validation, information, context, and decision-making.

I had a faulty belief that the information I needed to make my life decisions were OUT THERE rather than within me.

5. *I let fear and doubt run the show for too long.* Even when I contemplated a change, I let fear shut it down before I had the chance to process it or explore it or get curious about it. I have come to learn that I feel uncomfortable and fearful when I'm up to something good.

Work is such an important—but often stressful and contentious—part of our lives. How would you describe your relationship with work right now? With ambition? With productivity?

Mine may always be a complicated one. But one thing always remains true: *Everywhere I go, there I am.* I am the creator of the business goals; I am the owner of my calendar and yet—if I'm not careful—I find myself in hyper-productivity all over again, creating conditions that interfere with other areas of my life.

As we all know, work is such a crucial part of our lives. I know I spent many years working *so hard* toward goals that weren't mine, that weren't necessarily aligned to what really had meaning and sig- nificance to me. I worked at jobs that made use of skills I wasn't really that thrilled to put into practice.

It was only when I took stock of what *really* mattered to me—and took a stand for how I *really* wanted to experience my life—that I then had true clarity on what needed to change and what I needed to create. There were tough conversations and tough decisions. But finally, I am living a life of my own design.

Productivity, goals, and ambition are still present. And I can sometimes get hooked into workaholism and productivity, but now I know what to look out for, how to catch myself when I'm slipping into old behavior, and how to reconnect with my own inner truth. Sometimes I do a better job at this than others. I'm a work in progress—and I think I always will be—but it starts with connecting to myself, slowing down, honoring my boundaries, and creating space for joy.

My hope and wish for you is that you can define success and balance for yourself—and create a life *by your own design*.

RESOURCES

Books

Brené Brown, *Atlas of the Heart,* 2021

Brené Brown, *Dare to Lead,* 2018

Brené Brown, *The Gifts of Imperfection,* 2010

Beatrice Chestnut, *The Complete Enneagram*, 2013

Beatrice Chestnut & Uranio Paes, *The Enneagram of Waking Up,* 2021

James Clear, *Atomic Habits,* 2018

Danielle LaPorte, *Desire Map,* 2014

Tara Mohr, *Playing Big*, 2015

Websites

stephaniewoodward.com

agencytochange.com

feelingswheel.com

https://store.hbr.org/product/

for-real-productivity-less-is-truly-more/H006B8

Harvard Business Review, "For real productivity, less is truly more," by Tony Schwartz, May 17, 2010

ACKNOWLEDGMENTS

To the YGT team, thank you! To Sabrina for always bringing positivity and optimism to a process that can feel so stressful, *thank you*. And to Kelly, Doris, Christine, and Michelle for turning my manuscript into a physical book that I'm now holding in my hand.

To K.J., you know what you did ☺. Thank you for blessing me with your genius in my moment of panic.

To Chris K-F. and Firefly, this manuscript was born at a Firefly retreat in Northern Ontario. My Firefly experience is what brought me back to writing as an adult. I can't thank you enough for creating the writing spaces that you do.

To Kelsi M. for the hot tub conversations that led to big creative output.

To my biggest book cheerleaders for the past six-plus years—Danelle (you get the gold medal cheerleading award, btw), Allison, Tara, Lindsay B., Lindsay C., Cora, Steph G., Laurie F, Xander (I promised I'd write you into the book—here you go), Jackie, Ken, Courtney, Zach,

Sawyer, Julie, Caroline, Suzie, and Romina. Every time you asked me about the book or cheered my progress, you gave me the fuel I needed to keep going (and not let myself off the hook!).

To Leslie and Sam for just being awesome friends and supporters—I always know I can turn to you for an honest perspective. You're part of my "square" people.

To Kim C. for being my operational advisor, chief pacesetter, and friend for the last two years, holding me accountable to manage myself as a resource and stay focused on what *really* mattered.

To Alyssa for being my very first reader, giving me great support and feedback, and listening to me talk for endless hours about this book. It's shocking to me that you've only been in my life for a few years—you're stuck with me now for lifelong friendship.

To Carolyn, who encouraged me to take that final step to get published and for being a trusted sounding board (and ear to freak out to) throughout this process. And for being both an awesome business partner *and* awesome friend.

To Ileana and Sara for being die-hard friends through and through.

To Shea, while you're not named in this book, you are also a critical part of this story (just too young to give proper consent to be in the printed version!). I'm thankful every day that you came into my life.

To Mum and Sher for living through all of this life story right alongside me. (Sher, notice the memories don't start until you're in the picture ☺). We're a small family, but a mighty one.

And, finally, to Terry. Thank you for showing up in my life at exactly the right time and for being exactly who you are. Thank you for building our dream northern getaway—where so many of these manuscript words were written. And thank you for never (okay, *rarely*) questioning my endless hours in writer's pose. And for passing me all those coffees and breakfast sandwiches (just to be clear: there's no need for that to stop now that the book is done!).

YGTMedia Co. is a blended boutique publishing house for mission-driven humans. We help seasoned and emerging authors "birth their brain babies" through a supportive and collaborative approach. Specializing in narrative nonfiction and adult and children's empowerment books, we believe that words can change the world, and we intend to do so one book at a time.

 ygtmedia.co/publishing

 @ygtmedia.company

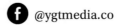 @ygtmedia.co

Manufactured by Amazon.ca
Bolton, ON

29270047R00164